THE OFFICIAL
COMPANION
SEASON TWO

El Giftaid

BATTLESTAR GALACTICA:
THE OFFICIAL COMPANION SEASON TWO

ISBN: 1 84576 221 5
ISBN-13: 978 1 84576 221 6

Published by
Titan Books
A division of
Titan Publishing Group Ltd
144 Southwark Street
London SE1 0UP

First edition August 2006
2 4 6 8 10 9 7 5 3 1

ACKNOWLEDGEMENTS

The author would like to thank the cast and crew of *Battlestar Galactica* not only for their extensive and insightful input into this book, but also for producing another superlative year of TV drama. Special praise must go to the series' guiding lights, Ron Moore and David Eick, and the show's writing staff, plus Mary McDonnell for penning her wonderful foreword.

A full-gun Colonial salute also goes to the extraordinary work of unit publicist Carol Marks-George, plus the similarly exemplary efforts of Maril Davis and James Halpern at Universal and Lana Kim at Sci Fi. Further kudos belongs to Cindy Chang, Gary Lokum and Dawn Rosenquist at Universal Licensing, Josef Fergusen and Mike Gibson.

At Titan, I'd like to offer my sincere thanks to my superb editor Jo Boylett, plus her esteemed colleagues Adam Newell and Cath Trechman. I must also pay tribute to Katy Wild, David 'Baz' Barraclough and Bob Kelly at Titan Books and Sharon Gosling, Ned Hartley and Brian J. Robb at *Battlestar Galactica Magazine* for their continued support of this book series, as well as Martin Stiff for his design work.

On a personal note, I'd like to thank Ian Calcutt, Toby Weidmann, Rich Matthews, Matt Chapman and Jayne Nelson for their thoughts and encouragement. I'm also grateful to Joan and Joanna Martin-Kaye for their constant kindness and support, while my beloved wife Jayne continues to light my way like a map to Earth.

DEDICATION

For my parents, Tessa and Mike, and my brother, Danny — three shining stars of my life.

Visit our website:
www.titanbooks.com

Did you enjoy this book? We love to hear from our readers. Please email us at:
readerfeedback@titanemail.com or write to Reader Feedback at the above address.

To subscribe to our regular newsletter for up-to-the-minute news, great offers and competitions,
email: **titan-news@titanemail.com**

A CIP catalogue record for this title is available from the British Library.

Printed and bound in Canada.

THE OFFICIAL
COMPANION
SEASON TWO

DAVID BASSOM

TITAN BOOKS

[CONTENTS]

R eally, when it comes down to it, if you're lucky, your career as an actor has within it several projects along the way that bring you peace.

When David Bassom asked me to write something for *Battlestar Galactica: The Official Companion Season Two*, I was getting ready to begin work on season three. I'd been noticing the subtle energetic shift as I opened back up to the character of Laura Roslin. Someone once asked me, "What happens to Laura when Mary is on hiatus?" I answered, "She's resting." So I'd like to thank David for this delightful opportunity to reflect on *Battlestar* and in the process bring Laura out of her repose.

I remember my first read of Ron Moore's brilliant miniseries, *Battlestar Galactica*. I remember closing the script quietly, and laying it down gently on the dresser in my bedroom. I sat very still in an old white Queen Anne chair. The house was silent; I could hear a lawnmower or a leaf blower or a buzz saw or something, somewhere in the background.

The feeling was one I have experienced four or five times in my career of twenty-five years. It was a kind of delicious mixture of excitement, fear and relief. The excitement rose from having been taken on a beautifully articulated, suspenseful and emotionally satisfying journey. The fear was a direct result of the dawning realization that I was going to have to actually do this project. And doing the project would mean leaving home and rearranging my cellular activity (or so it seemed) in order to respond to a completely different world, different set of circumstances and new group of intimates. The relief was by far the most gratifying. A rare sensation of peaceful wellbeing came over me.

Actors spend their lives searching for worlds they can enter, searching for stories that require their particular talents, their ideas, their idiosyncrasies. We search for involvement in stories that contain relevance to our world, because built deeply into the core impulses of the actor is a strong, almost overwhelming need to connect with the people. Owing to the reading of the script of *Battlestar* that evening my life shifted in the silence and I entered a brazen, challenging and completely beguiling new world. A world that, due to my great good fortune, required me. For that moment the actor's search was over.

Filming the miniseries coincided with the US invasion of Iraq. I remember coming back to my hotel room from the set and sitting up till the early morning hours watching CNN. This was the beginning of an experience of an almost seamless synchronistic chronicling of our times. From the very beginning acting in *Battlestar* often felt more like a mission or a deployment (bar the star trailer — and you would have to kill me before I'd give it up — and the first-class catering) than a career in the entertainment industry. For Laura in the miniseries, the overriding internal issue was the constant negotiation of her liberal impulses versus the realities of survival on a tribal level. It required from me, playing President Roslin, a deliberate surrender to the idea of the use of force as a way of accomplishing a greater good; a future.

Reflecting on season one I experience a blur of intrigue and survival. Inside our lives on the ships it literally felt like we would crack. Every event contained within it a sensation of ultimate and potentially irrevocable consequence. The environment was one of

relentlessly high stakes that required precise action. Everything an actor wants or needs in order to play well was close at hand, including an extraordinarily devoted and talented crew. It is something close to awe that I feel when I reflect on the keen interpretive and steadfast presence of Steve McNutt and his camera crew. They are the constant for the actors. They've been there for every moment of discovery, every difficulty, every instance of exposure. They have profoundly contributed to the most essential element of getting good work from actors: trust.

The end of season one came so quickly the experience still felt new. Even though the material was always changing and always surprising, it contained an uncanny logic. The President ending up in jail seemed as reasonable and necessary by the time it came as Laura taking the oath of office had in the miniseries.

As opposed to the claustrophobic airless experience of season one, my image of season two is expansion. We encountered new ships, visited old worlds and finally settled for a moment on land. Laura faced difficult decisions requiring a ruthlessness so underdeveloped in me that I doubted it every step of the way (a special thanks to David Eick, who possesses a skillful and humorous way of convincing me of the necessity of the most dastardly deeds).

By the end of season two, we had indeed been through it all together. As a company we had succeeded in achieving the highest of accolades that Broadcast Television awards, the Peabody. AFI honored *Battlestar Galactica*, acknowledging it as soaring "light years beyond the expectations of science fiction on television". And *Time* magazine named *Battlestar* the number one show on television.

Now on the set there is an air of confidence, familiarity and deeply, deeply felt gratitude among the hundreds involved. We have returned for season three intact with the blazing talents of Michael Rymer, Sergio, Ed (my dashing partner in crime), Jamie, Katee, James, Tricia, Grace, Michael, Aaron, Tahmoh, Alessandro, Kandyse, Nicki and all, Harvey, Glenne, Michelle, Gerald and the entire exceptional crew of *Battlestar*.

Judging by the first *Official Companion*, I have tremendous confidence in the quality of what you are about to read. David Bassom and Titan Books understand and beautifully enhance the world of *Battlestar Galactica*. I hope you enjoy reading it and thank you for giving me the opportunity to talk about a project I so dearly love.

Mary McDonnell
May 2006

[SECOND CHANCES]

MingWei
The Whale Kingdom Quest

---

186 CONTINUED: 186

> ADAMA
> Congratulations, Lieutenant.
> You carried out a difficult and
> dangerous mission… and you did it
> despite whatever personal misgivings
> you may or may not have had.

That was meant for Lee, and he knows it.

> ADAMA (cont'd)
> I'm proud of you.

> SHARON
> Thank you, sir.

Adama puts out a hand for Sharon. But instead of shaking his
hand, Sharon pulls her weapon and SHOOTS ADAMA IN THE CHEST.

Adama hits the floor. Everyone stands stock still for a beat
-- then Lee rushes across the room and is the first one to
reach his father.

As Lee rolls him over and cradles him in his arms, BLOOD SOAKING
his uniform…

FADE TO BLACK.

END OF ACT FOUR

[SECOND CHANCES]

"In season two, we set out to expand and deepen the storytelling. We also wanted to send our characters into different directions and just subvert the audience's expectations whenever possible."

— Ronald D. Moore

After successfully plotting a new course for episodic science-fiction television, the first season of *Battlestar Galactica* concluded with a shattering cliffhanger that had all the explosive impact of a Cylon nuke. The closing moments of season one's thirteenth and final episode, 'Kobol's Last Gleaming, Part II', left Commander William Adama fighting for his life, President Laura Roslin behind bars, Captain Lee 'Apollo' Adama under arrest, Lieutenant Kara 'Starbuck' Thrace on Caprica and various other characters, including Vice President Gaius Baltar and Chief Tyrol, facing bleak futures on Kobol. Clearly, it was an extraordinary end to an extraordinary season of science-fiction drama — and an end that left the audience hungry for more *Battlestar Galactica*.

Fortunately, viewers wouldn't have to wait too long for the continuation of the Colonials' struggle for survival. The resounding critical and commercial success of season one's première airing in the UK and US led to *Battlestar Galactica* being officially renewed for a second season by the US Sci Fi Channel, Universal Television and the UK's Sky TV on February 9 2005, just weeks after season one's US début.

By the time *Battlestar Galactica*'s renewal was announced, head writer/executive producer Ronald D. Moore and executive producer David Eick had already spent more than two months developing their plans for season two. They had also formed a clear idea of what they wanted to accomplish with the series' second year.

"Our main goal for season two was to avoid the sophomore slump," says Moore. "We wanted to maintain the quality of the show and live up to what the first season and the miniseries had done. We wanted to take where we were at the end of 'Kobol's Last Gleaming, Part II' and keep going in that direction, and really just build on all our strengths."

"We always wanted season two to continue to push the show in unusual directions and keep it risky and bold rather than just play by the usual rules of ongoing television," Eick adds. "We definitely wanted to delve more deeply into the emotional points-of-view of our antagonists and explore even more of the shortcomings and character flaws of our protagonists — and those are not things you normally do on television."

Moore and Eick began working on season two's storylines shortly after principal photography wrapped on season one in September 2004. Their first meeting took place at the informal setting of Firefly restaurant in Studio City, California, where *Battlestar Galactica*'s guiding lights casually discussed early concepts for the season's story arc and plotlines over dinner and several glasses of Scotch whisky.

"Season two began with David and I talking about some basic ideas," explains Moore, "like how long it was going to take to get the family of characters back together, how Adama's shooting would affect him and how the characters were going to find a map to Earth. We talked about all that at length and then briefed the network on our general game-plan for season two and got their thoughts on it, before we took it to the writing staff."

"We were given a pretty free rein in the development of season two," Eick continues. "I think the network's only real concern at the beginning — and it was a concern we all shared — had to do with the extent to which we had split the cast between the *Galactica*, Caprica and Kobol. At one point we toyed with going for the first eight or ten episodes like that, but I think we quickly realized neither we nor the audience wanted to be without Edward James Olmos [as Commander Adama] for that long. As determined as we were to maintain the reality of what had happened to Adama and avoid him being back in action in the first episode, we also appreciated we didn't want to prolong that to an unnecessarily long degree."

While the development of season one had largely been based on the ideas contained in his Series Bible, Moore decided against penning an internal writers' guide for season two. Instead, he wanted the freedom to see what storylines and character arcs naturally developed in the writers' meetings.

Above: While the premises of the opening installments of season two were conceived by Ronald D. Moore and David Eick, other episodes like 'The Farm' were conceptualised during meetings of the show's entire writing staff.

"Our initial discussions were all about how we were going to resolve all the storylines from the cliffhanger in a five- or six-episode arc, which ultimately became a seven-episode arc," Moore recalls. "We talked about all the plotlines for those episodes and didn't really discuss other storylines at that point.

"When we started having those discussions, I already knew I wanted certain things: I wanted Tigh to be in charge of the fleet for a few episodes, I wanted Adama to be in a coma for a few episodes and I wanted Tigh's management of the fleet to be a disaster that would spark a rebellion and prompt Laura to break out of jail aided by Lee in some way. I knew there would then be a split in the fleet and that Laura would decide to go back to Kobol and Adama would come back to command at around the same time. That was sort of the sketch of what we wanted to do. But episodes like 'The Farm', which had Kara down on Caprica, and 'Fragged', which concerned what happened to the people on Kobol, really came out of the writers' room; I don't think we had generalized ideas for what was going to happen there."

Once ideas for the season's opening story arc had been finalized, *Battlestar Galactica*'s writing staff would proceed to develop the rest of season two's first half, starting with the cliffhanging tenth episode that would temporarily halt Sci Fi's broadcast of the season. This episode quickly became 'Pegasus', a reworking of the original *Battlestar Galactica* two-parter 'The Living Legend', that introduced a second surviving Battlestar, the *Pegasus*. "The arrival of the *Pegasus* was an obvious candidate for the mid-season cliffhanger," explains Moore. "As soon as the idea came up, we all gravitated towards it.

"We didn't really think about the last ten episodes of the season till later on," he adds. "It was during the development of those episodes that we came up with the majority of things that lead to the finale."

During the conception of the season's episodes, the show's writers found that plotlines were normal-

Above: Season two's tenth episode, 'Pegasus', was devised as a reworking of the original series' two-part adventure, 'The Living Legend'.

ly inspired by character developments rather than high-concept premises. "Our story-lines didn't start with us saying, 'Okay, who comes to bother the *Galactica* this week and what do the crew do about it?' or 'What does the *Galactica* crew have to destroy this week to maintain its survival?'" Eick recalls. "Much more often the stories started with a character and us saying things like, 'What's happening with Sharon right now?' 'What's going on in Adama's mind?' 'How committed is Lee to his role as the CAG [Commander Air Group]?' 'How does Laura feel about this trek through mysticism?' These sorts of things became the catalysts for stories, rather than the mission-of-the-week."

From the start of the season's development, it was agreed that season two would not set out to produce any comedy-orientated episodes. Although *Battlestar Galactica* had experimented in this area during season one with the episodes 'Six Degrees of Separation' and, most notably, 'Tigh Me Up, Tigh Me Down', season two would concentrate on dramatic scenarios.

"Whenever you're doing the first season of a show, you have to find the show's breadth, its tonal elasticity," says Eick. "You just don't know it until you've tried certain things. I think the 'Tigh Me Up, Tigh Me Down' episode, with its kind of wacky Blake Edwards-style rhythm, just doesn't suit the environment of the show. Eddie Olmos, as a director, found a way to make that episode work, but going in that comedy direction threatens to take viewers out of the tactile realism the show has created and make you feel you're not watching *Battlestar Galactica* any more."

"It's important to have humor in the show, but I don't think we should do entire episodes that are tongue in cheek," Moore agrees. "I don't feel that fits the show too well."

Above and opposite: Season two's story arc depicted Gaius Baltar's emergence as a darker and more dangerous character, and also followed the drama surrounding the arrival of Sharon Valerii's human-Cylon baby.

For season two, *Battlestar Galactica*'s existing writing staff of Toni Graphia, David Weddle, Bradley Thompson and Carla Robinson was augmented at various points by a number of other scribes, all of whom were chosen for their sense of dramatic and character-driven storytelling rather than their knowledge of space opera. The list of newcomers was headed by veteran writer/producer Mark Verheiden (whose many credits include *Smallville*, the movie *The Mask*, and both the *Timecop* film and its TV spin-off) and rising writer Anne Cofell Saunders (*24*).

"Mark Verheiden was someone who came highly recommended," Moore recalls. "He had spent many years on various other television shows. He came in and clearly had great organizational skills, and was also a good writer. It was a good fit because we needed a really solid person to come in and help me out by running the writers' room, because I had a lot of other things to do at the same time.

"Anne was a real discovery. She had done an episode of *24* and had been an assistant over there, and they really thought very highly of her. She did a great job with the first draft of 'Pegasus', so we kept her on staff."

The other additions to the writing staff for parts of season two were Joel Anderson Thompson and the writing team of Dawn Prestwich and Nicole Yorkin. "Joel was someone else who came highly recommended," says Moore. "He wrote a great *Boomtown*

Above: 'The Captain's Hand' was the third episode of *Battlestar Galactica* to be scripted by freelance writer Jeff Vlaming.

episode David and I read and really loved. We met him and he was really engaging and really interesting, and he was really smart in the writers' room. Joel provided a great deal of insight, and a lot of the better ideas in the writers' room came from his mouth.

"Dawn and Nicole were people I had worked with on *Carnivale* and I liked them a lot. They were senior level writers and had great instincts in terms of characters and emotion."

Towards the end of production on season two, Moore recruited a freelance writer to script an episode — namely Jeff Vlaming, who had previously penned the first season installments 'Litmus' and 'Tigh Me Up, Tigh Me Down'. "I asked Jeff to write another episode for us because we reached a point where everyone on staff was busy on rewrites and new drafts and we needed a new person to step in and help us out," Moore reveals. "Jeff, by luck, happened to visit my office just as we were facing this problem and I said, 'Hey Jeff! How are you? Want to do a script?' And he said 'Sure'!"

In a change from season one (which boasted four scripts credited to the series' developer), Moore would only be named as the scriptwriter of one second season installment and the co-writer of two other episodes. "I only take credit on episodes where I do the first draft," he explains, "that's my internal rule on the show. And I didn't assign myself a lot of first drafts on season two, primarily because I had so much else to do. But I still took a [re-writing] pass at every single episode of the season."

All of season one's principal department heads returned for *Battlestar Galactica*'s second season, including producer Harvey Frand, production designer Richard Hudolin, visual effects supervisor Gary Hutzel and costume designer Glenne Campbell. The show's seven primary cast members were also confirmed in their roles, along with the majority of the series' supporting players.

"In most cases, we already had the actors tied to five-year or six-year contracts," explains Eick. "There were some actors at the start of season two that hadn't been tied up because we didn't know enough about them as characters or as actors when we started the show, so we embarked on making serious deals with them. That took some doing because by that point the actors and their agents clearly knew we wanted them! But we were able to get everyone we wanted: we got Michael Hogan [Colonel Tigh], Aaron Douglas [Chief Tyrol], Tahmoh Penikett [Lieutenant Karl 'Helo' Agathon], Nicki Clyne

TITLE SEQUENCE: GALACTICA

Battlestar *Galactica*'s title sequence was the subject of some modifications during the series' second season. Season two's title sequence featured the theme music from the original, UK-broadcast season one title sequence, but initially dropped the collection of clips from the upcoming episode that previously formed the closing part of the title sequence.

"We went back to the title music Ron and I originally wanted," explains Eick, "and we agreed to omit the clips because there was some concern about the amount of time that went by between the teaser and the start of act one [due to the advertising break on US broadcasts]. But we always felt the clips were really valuable to the show — they're a good way to hook audience members and keep them watching — so we were really pleased when Mark Stern from Sci Fi called us and asked to get them put back from episode five."

Season two's title sequence also incorporates on-screen text references to the quest for Earth and the number of survivors on that quest. "I think the reference to Earth came about because the network wanted us to set up the premise of the show and the characters' goal a bit more clearly," Moore recalls. "It was [associate producer] Paul Leonard's idea to mention the number of survivors and change the number each week. It was a great idea."

"I felt that changing the number of survivors would engage the fans and bring another element of reality to the humans' struggle," reveals Leonard, who is personally responsible for calculating the survivor total shown each week. "I go through the episodes with the editors and attempt to count the casualties from dog fights, explosions, etc. I then send a list to David and Ron with that headcount, along with my reasoning. They augment it by adjusting the number slightly to suggest deaths by illness or births not featured in the show. The number of survivors only reflects the headcount in the fleet." ■

[Cally], Alessandro Juliani [Gaeta], Kandyse McClure [Dualla] and, to an extent, Paul Campbell [Billy Keikeya]."

One actor who wasn't signed up for season two, however, was Connor Widdows. Boxey became the first 'victim' of season two when Moore decided that the *Galactica*'s most famous child resident was no longer a necessary part of the series. "We just didn't find good roles for Boxey in the show," Moore admits. "We talked about using him as the 'Artful Dodger' in season one and kept finding little storylines to weave him into, but we then kept finding his scenes were always the most 'cut-able' parts of the episodes. It wasn't something anyone really sparked to. We were never really happy with the little storylines we came up with for Boxey and we had so many other characters that he became someone who fell by the wayside."

At least Boxey was merely written out of the series. Four other supporting characters found themselves marked for death during season two: Socinus (who is killed off in 'Valley of Darkness'), Alex 'Crashdown' Quartararo (who makes his last appearance in 'Fragged'), Elosha (who dies in 'Home, Part I') and the previously mentioned Billy Keikeya (who was killed off towards the end of the season, in 'Sacrifice').

"If you are willing to let familiar characters die, it puts genuine jeopardy into situations," says Moore of the four characters' demises. "But above all, the deaths of those characters helped provide us with compelling stories."

Another casualty of season two was Lieutenant Sharon 'Boomer' Valerii. As part of the series' ongoing mission to defy viewers' expectations, Moore decided that the original 'Boomer Sharon' — rather than the duplicitous 'Caprica Sharon' — would be killed off, and initially toyed with having Chief Tyrol be responsible for her death, until Toni Graphia outlined an alternative plan in her script for 'Resistance'. Moore also chose to have Boomer's place on the *Galactica* taken by Caprica Sharon.

"I liked the transposition of the two," he explains. "I liked the idea of taking the Sharon we first met on Caprica and putting her on *Galactica*, and I liked taking our Boomer and putting her back with the Cylons. I thought it was interesting because they had conflicted reactions and emotions, but what was running through both of them was a sense of vulnerability."

One of Moore and Eick's general goals for *Battlestar Galactica*'s second season was to attract some famous actors to play guest roles in the series. This led to the casting of such stars as Lucy Lawless, Dana Delany, Dean Stockwell, Bill Duke and John Heard.

"You're always looking for 'name' guest stars when you're doing a show — they elevate the material and they bring an audience, so it's good for everyone," Moore notes. "In the first season it was harder to get those people because the show was much more of an unknown quantity — we were still trying to overcome the name of the show to try to get people to consider it. But by the time we reached the second season it had achieved a certain amount of success and critical acclaim and word was getting out into the community, so agents were more willing to approach their clients and say, 'We want to pitch you *Battlestar Galactica* and, before you say no, we want you to really give this a chance and

Opposite: Alex 'Crashdown' Quartararo was an early fatality of *Battlestar Galactica*'s second season.

here's why…' We found we had more doors open to us in the second season."

"Getting 'name' actors is a great way to get a show extra publicity and attract extra viewers," Eick agrees. "But we also knew we had to do it carefully, so it wouldn't betray the reality of the piece. We didn't want the guest actors to take viewers out of the show and make them go, 'Hey, look, there's Xena!' So we were very conscious that the guest casting had to be handled correctly."

The majority of season one's directors were invited back to helm episodes of *Battlestar Galactica*'s second season, together with three directors — Michael Nankin, James Head and Reynaldo Villalobos — who were new to the show. "From the beginning, we've always looked for directors whose work demonstrates they have a consistent ability to deliver good performances and tell stories with a lot of texture and depth," Eick notes. "We don't look for experienced sci-fi guys or action-adventure guys or space-adventure guys."

Reflecting Sci Fi, Sky and Universal's confidence in the series, *Battlestar Galactica* received an expanded twenty-episode order for its second season. The increased order clearly presented some pros and cons for the show's makers.

"I think the creative team would rather have done thirteen episodes, because you can focus on each episode more and you don't get the same exhaustion factor going," Moore admits. "But twenty is a more traditional number for television, it gets to that magic number for syndication quicker and the more episodes you have, the easier it is to amortize costs over the course of a season. There are a lot of reasons economically for going for

EXECUTIVE COMMENTARIES

Like the latter five episodes of season one, the US broadcasts of *Battlestar Galactica*'s second season were accompanied by exclusive podcasts recorded by Ronald D. Moore. Available for free download via the US Sci Fi Channel's website, these audio commentaries provide Moore with a chance to offer frank, fascinating and often funny insights into the making of the series.

"I enjoy recording the podcasts," says Moore. "I started recording them after Craig Engler at SciFi.com called me and asked if I'd be interested in doing them. I actually hadn't heard of podcasting when he first mentioned it to me, but I'd always enjoyed doing DVD commentaries and thought the podcast idea sounded like fun. It's great to put out a commentary on an episode at the same time the audience is seeing it rather than several months later, which is what happens with DVDs."

Further behind-the-scenes secrets about the making of season two were revealed on SciFi.com courtesy of David Eick's *Battlestar Galactica Video Blog*.

"I liked the idea of doing a video blog because I thought it would give the fans a different look at the process of making the show and possibly encourage some people to go into filmmaking," Eick reveals. "It was also a chance to be a bit silly. Ron and I do a lot of very serious interviews and commentaries for this show, so I see the video blog as an opportunity to take a different approach and really show the fun we have making the series." ∎

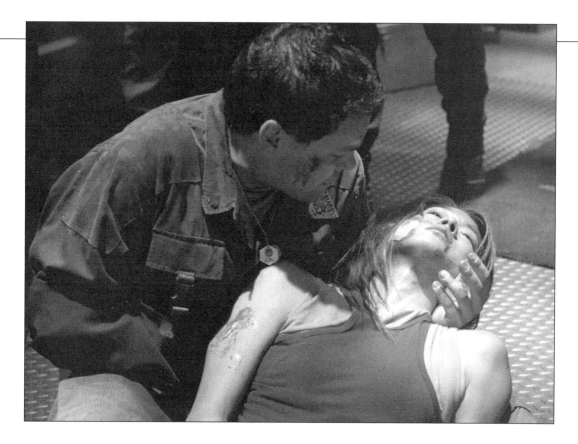

Above: Writer Toni Graphia came up with the idea of killing Sharon 'Boomer' Valerii while scripting 'Resistance'.

twenty over thirteen."

"From a business standpoint, I was certainly in favor of a twenty-episode order because the more episodes you do, the greater chance you have to expand your audience and become a fixture on people's television sets," Eick notes. "But on a personal level, sure, I think we would have preferred a thirteen-episode order. I would always prefer to work my ass off sixteen hours a day for six months of the year, rather than for nine months of the year!"

To alleviate the pressure, it was decided before season two entered production that shooting would be divided into two blocks. Following principal photography on the season's opening ten installments, production would take a month-long hiatus before resuming for the closing ten episodes.

"I think that idea came from something David discussed," Moore recalls. "It was something other series for USA Networks and Sci Fi had done and it was a good way to catch up on scripts. We knew Sci Fi was going to be splitting the broadcast of the season into two halves anyway, so it made our post-production period a little easier to deal with. It was just a good thing for everyone."

Season two of *Battlestar Galactica* began shooting on March 31 2005, in preparation for the season's US début on July 15. Principal photography began at the show's regular production base at Vancouver Film Studios, Canada. ■

[SEASON TWO]

The Cylons were created by Man.

They rebelled.

They evolved.

They look and feel Human.

Some are programmed to think they are Human.

There are many copies…

And they have a plan.

THE CAST

Commander William 'Husker' Adama: Edward James Olmos
President Laura Roslin: Mary McDonnell
Captain Lee 'Apollo' Adama: Jamie Bamber
Lt Kara 'Starbuck' Thrace: Katee Sackhoff
Dr Gaius Baltar: James Callis
Number Six: Tricia Helfer
Lt Sharon 'Boomer' Valerii/Number Eight: Grace Park
Colonel Saul Tigh: Michael Hogan
Chief Galen Tyrol: Aaron Douglas
Lt Karl 'Helo' Agathon: Tahmoh Penikett
Petty Officer 2nd Class Anastasia Dualla: Kandyse McClure
Lt Felix Gaeta: Alessandro Juliani
Cally: Nicki Clyne
Billy Keikeya: Paul Campbell (1-16)
Dr Cottle: Donnelly Rhodes (03, 04, 07, 08, 11-14, 17, 18, 20)
Lt Margaret 'Racetrack' Edmondson: Leah Cairns (01, 03, 04, 07-10, 13, 14, 19)
Tom Zarek: Richard Hatch (03-07, 14, 17, 19, 20)
Brendan 'Hotdog' Constanza: Bodie Olmos (01, 02, 04, 06, 08, 09, 13, 15)
Lt Louanne 'Kat' Katraine: Luciana Carro (01, 02, 06, 08, 11, 13, 15)
Ellen Tigh: Kate Vernon (01-04, 08, 16, 20)
Samuel T. Anders: Michael Trucco (04, 05, 18-20)

THE CREW

Developed by: Ronald D. Moore
Executive Producers: Ronald D. Moore and David Eick
Co-Executive Producers: Toni Graphia and Mark Verheiden (7-20)
Producer: Harvey Frand
Co-Producers: Bradley Thompson and David Weddle
Executive Story Editor: Joel Thompson
Story Editor: Carla Robinson
Consulting Producers: Mark Verheiden (1-6) and Glen A. Larson
Based on the series Battlestar Galactica created by:
Glen A. Larson
Production Designer: Richard Hudolin
Art Director: Douglas McLean
Visual Effects Supervisor: Gary Hutzel
Director of Photography: Stephen McNutt
Costume Designer: Glenne Campbell
Music: Bear McCreary

[SCATTERED]

WRITERS: Bradley Thompson & David Weddle
DIRECTOR: Michael Rymer

GUEST CAST: Sam Witwer (Alex 'Crashdown' Quartararo), Alonso Oyarzun (Socinus), Kerry Norton (Paramedic Layne Ishay), Kurt Evans (Paramedic Howard Kim), Chris Shields (Corporal Venner), Jennifer Halley (Seelix), Warren Christie (Tarn), Ty Olsson (Captain Kelly), Nicholas Treeshin (Sergeant Watkins), Michael Tayles (Flyboy), Aleks Paunovic (Marine Sgt Fischer)

"Where's the fleet?" — Colonel Saul Tigh

Fearing that Commander Adama's shooting by Sharon 'Boomer' Valerii represents the prelude to a full-scale Cylon attack, Colonel Tigh orders the Battlestar *Galactica* and the civilian fleet to make an emergency FTL Jump. Unfortunately, the Jump separates the *Galactica* from the fleet and its finest surgeon, Dr Cottle.

Reminded of his decades-long friendship with Adama and everything he learned from him, Tigh becomes desperate to relocate the fleet. After his brutal interrogation of Sharon reveals nothing, Tigh orders the *Galactica* crew to prepare to return to its pre-Jump position. Once there, Gaeta will temporarily network the *Galactica*'s computers in a move that will allow the crew to locate the fleet but will also make the Battlestar susceptible to Cylon interference.

As the *Galactica*'s crew prepares to face the Cylons once again, the surviving members of their survey party continue to fight for their lives on the surface of Kobol. With Socinus' condition continuing to deteriorate, Alex 'Crashdown' Quartararo orders Tarn to retrace the group's steps and find a lost medkit. Joined by Chief Tyrol and Cally, Tarn successfully retrieves the medkit, but is killed shortly after by Cylon Centurions.

Meanwhile, on Cylon-occupied Caprica, Karl 'Helo' Agathon attempts to convince Kara 'Starbuck' Thrace that Sharon can be trusted. But before he can make any progress, Sharon steals Kara's Cylon Raider and flees.

Briefly returning to the vicinity of Kobol, the *Galactica* faces a heavy Cylon assault before it successfully locates and rejoins the fleet. Unbeknown to its crew, however, the *Galactica* is secretly boarded by Cylon Centurions during the attack...

Before 'Scattered' became the opening episode of *Battlestar Galactica*'s second season, Ronald D. Moore had other plans for the season première. "'Scattered' was originally going to be episode two," Moore reveals. "I initially didn't want to start the season by doing a direct pick-up from the season one cliffhanger; I wanted to subvert viewers' expectations by doing something a little different and not come back to the cliffhanger at all in episode one. So I pitched an episode to the network that I planned to write, which

was a story set before the attack on Caprica that was told from Adama's point of view.

"Ultimately, after talking to the network, we decided we didn't want to open the season that way. So we just sort of set that episode aside and moved 'Scattered' forward to give the season a more traditional pick-up from the cliffhanger."

The central premise of 'Scattered' actually began life long before *Battlestar Galactica*'s first season entered production, as Moore had first pitched an episode involving the *Galactica* being separated from the fleet when the network and studio were considering commissioning the weekly series. The storyline was assigned to the writing team of Bradley Thompson and David Weddle, who proceeded to combine it with the various unresolved plot threads from the end of season one to form season two's opener.

"The idea that Tigh manages to lose the fleet was something that Ron wanted to do, but we had no idea how to make it plausible," Thompson reveals. "It took several long sessions with Kevin Grazier, our JPL Cassini technical advisor, to figure out how Tigh could plausibly do it in a way that fit the plot elements we wanted to play with — for example, what would force the *Galactica* to go back to where they were to figure out where the fleet went?"

Above: The flashback sequences allowed *Battlestar Galactica* to explore the long friendship between William Adama and Saul Tigh.

As Thompson and Weddle's script took shape, Moore's request for an extra layer of character depth and personal drama prompted the writers to script some flashbacks to Adama and Tigh's past. "Toni Graphia had long advocated doing a flashback story where we would learn how Tigh and Adama became friends and brought the idea up again when we were working on 'Scattered'," Weddle recalls. "The flashbacks also gave us a way to show why the scattering of the fleet weighed so heavily on Tigh, and why it was so important personally for him to save the fleet. They would show that Adama had redeemed Tigh and rescued him from an emotional abyss."

A further benefit of employing flashbacks was that they allowed the show's leading man to play a key role in the episode. "Without the flashbacks, Adama was lying in a hospital bed, comatose, and one of our most powerful actors had nothing to do," Weddle agrees. "So that played a role in the decision to investigate the back-story of Tigh and Adama and the core of their relationship."

After Thompson and Weddle completed their last draft of the script for 'Scattered', Moore added the episode's final flashback to a drunken Tigh learning that Adama has arranged for him to return to service. "Ron felt a climactic scene was needed in which we actually see Adama rescue Tigh from an emotional low point, where he is hovering on the edge of self destruction," explains Weddle.

The task of bringing 'Scattered' to the screen was assigned to *Battlestar Galactica*'s principal director, Michael Rymer. While Rymer had previously directed the miniseries and three key episodes of the first series, he found that 'Scattered' presented several unique challenges. "The main problem with 'Scattered' was that it wasn't really beginning or ending a story," he notes. "The episode doesn't work that well as a stand-alone piece, but I think it works well as part of the ongoing storyline.

"There are a lot of great moments and scenes in the episode," he continues. "I think Michael Hogan and AJ [Alessandro Juliani] are terrific. The scene with Tigh interrogating Sharon is wonderful; Michael and Grace [Park] both really went for it. I thought the Kobol stuff looked great. And I loved the scene with Tigh trying to burn his medals; I thought that was very atmospheric."

"'Scattered' was, in many ways, the highlight of the season for me," says Michael Hogan of the episode. "I was surprised by its storyline — I thought Adama could have been back on his feet by the magic of television at the start of the episode. It was a challenging episode for me, as an actor, but it was a lot of fun, especially shooting the flashbacks with Edward James Olmos."

Hogan's appreciation for the episode's flashback sequences is shared by his co-star. "Those scenes were very rewarding to play and they helped the season really take off," Olmos notes.

SURVEILLANCE: ADDITIONAL

In writing the flashbacks to Adama and Tigh's lives following the Cylon War, David Weddle and Bradley Thompson drew on personal experience. "Brad and I are both the sons of war veterans," explains Weddle. "My father was a Marine in World War II and he fought in some of the most horrific battles of the South Pacific, including Guadalcanal and Okinawa. I watched first-hand how he struggled with his traumatic memories of that conflict and saw how they haunted him. So we wanted to show Tigh and Adama as veterans of the first Cylon war who were out of the service and having trouble adjusting."

"By going back in time and seeing how these people were, I think we enlightened viewers; viewers got to understand the characters more and feel for them more. You get to understand Adama and Tigh and their relationship better through those flashbacks. So I thought the flashbacks were revealing and they were also fun for us to shoot.

"I don't think the make-up worked too well, though," adds Olmos with a grin. "I don't think we could push back the amount of years they wanted to push back."

A variety of looks were considered for the younger Adama and Tigh (including, at one point, long hair and a handlebar moustache for the latter), before their appearances were settled on. The actors' 'rejuvenation' was later aided in post-production by the visual effects department.

"We made the frames thinner for those sequences," explains Gary Hutzel. "We squashed the frames by between ten and fifteen per cent, to try to make the actors look younger. We talked about doing other things like wrinkle removal, but because a lot of the flashbacks didn't make the finished cut we didn't feel it was necessary."

The visual effects department's other main contribution to 'Scattered' concerned the episode's climatic effects sequence, which included viewers' first look at the newly-designed Cylon Heavy Raider and the *Galactica*'s protective flak field. "I was very happy with that sequence, especially because of the flak field," says Hutzel. "I'd wanted to show the *Galactica* being protected by this stream of shrapnel from the start of the series and we finally got to do it in 'Scattered'."

Above: Colonel Tigh's ruthless interrogation of Sharon Valerii proved to be one of the season premiere's most memorable scenes.

Following the end of shooting, 'Scattered' went through further changes before the episode was completed. Rymer's initial cut of the episode removed all the flashback material, a small part of which was then reinstated by Moore.

"Without the flashbacks, the episode became an action piece and I felt it lacked heart and emotional depth and complexity," explains Moore. "So we came up with a way of using some of the flashback material we had in a way that related more to Tigh and his experiences in the episode. The episode is ultimately a character study of Tigh and a look at his relationship with Adama." ∎

[VALLEY OF DARKNESS]

WRITERS: Bradley Thompson & David Weddle
DIRECTOR: Michael Rymer

GUEST CAST: Sam Witwer (Alex 'Crashdown' Quartararo), Alonso Oyarzun (Socinus), Kerry Norton (Paramedic Layne Ishay), Chris Shields (Corporal Venner), Jennifer Halley (Seelix), Ty Olsson (Captain Kelly), Michael Tayles (Flyboy), Dominic Zamprogna (Jammer), Garvin Cross (Ray Collishaw), Brad Loree (Phil Bonnington), Lori Stewart (Twinam)

> "Get to Aft Damage Control and get there right frakking now, mister! Get there before the Cylons or we lose the ship..."
> — Colonel Tigh, to Captain Lee Adama

While trying to cleanse the Battlestar's systems of the remains of a Cylon computer virus, the *Galactica*'s crew becomes aware that the ship has been boarded by a Cylon landing party. Based on his previous encounter with the Cylons when they invaded the *Brennok* during the first Cylon War, Colonel Tigh immediately recognizes the landing party's plan. He tells the *Galactica*'s crew that they must stop the Centurions from venting the Battlestar's air supply and then turning the ship's guns on the rest of the fleet.

Tigh orders a small group of marines led by Captain Lee Adama to stop the Centurions from reaching Aft Damage Control. After rushing to the aid of President Roslin, Billy and Dualla, Adama's group manages to destroy the Cylon landing party in a fierce battle.

Back on Kobol, Chief Tyrol and Cally rejoin the other survivors only to discover that they are too late to save Socinus. Tyrol can do nothing for his dying friend other than give him a lethal injection to end his pain.

Stranded with them, Gaius Baltar continues to have disturbing visions and hallucinates Commander Adama killing the human-Cylon child that Number Six says he is destined to protect. Baltar also learns more about the dark acts that once occurred on Kobol.

Far away, on Cylon-occupied Caprica, Kara Thrace visits her old apartment with Karl Agathon. After a brief rest, they leave the area in her pick-up truck...

'Valley of Darkness' was developed as the second installment of *Battlestar Galactica*'s second season after it became clear that there were too many plotlines and events in 'Scattered' to be contained in one episode. "When we turned in our second writers' draft of 'Scattered', Michael Rymer said, 'There's so much good material here, instead of cutting the script down, why not expand it into a two-parter?'" recalls David Weddle, who scripted both of season two's opening episodes with longtime writing partner Bradley Thompson. "We were more than happy to do that, but we also knew that meant we had

Above: Many of the events in 'Valley of
Darkness' were originally scripted
to take place in the second-season opener,
'Scattered'.

to come up with additional material so the second script didn't feel padded. So Brad and
I came up with the idea of Cylon Centurions boarding the *Galactica* and a battle inside
the ship from corridor to corridor.

"We pitched that to Ron Moore and David Eick, and their eyes lit up like hundred-
watt bulbs. They said, 'Yes, let's go for it!'"

"That episode gave us a chance to do the James Cameron movie *Aliens* on *Battlestar
Galactica*," adds David Eick with a grin. "It was a fun idea, but when we got into actually doing it, the planning it required was huge! Fortunately, we managed to work
through it all and I think Gary Hutzel and the effects team did some great stuff with
the Centurions."

Jamie Bamber was thrilled to discover the episode required Lee Adama to lead the
fight against the *Galactica*'s invading Cylons Centurions — who, of course, were actually computer-generated characters that were added into the scenes during post-production. "I enjoyed shooting those sequences because I'd always wanted my character to
come face-to-face with a Cylon Centurion," explains Bamber. "It was a fun acting

Above: Commander Adama's shocking execution of the Cylon baby was one of the most controversial moments of season two.

exercise to imagine them in the scene with me as I fired at them and responded to them jumping at me!"

While the episode's main plotline concerned the crew's battle with the Cylons, much of 'Valley of Darkness' was devoted to continuing the ongoing Kobol storyline. Weddle and Thompson strove to make the survivors' exploits on Kobol as gritty and believable as they possibly could.

"When it fell upon us to write season two's opening chapters of that Kobol storyline, we were determined to bring a level of visceral reality to them that is usually absent from sci-fi shows," Weddle notes. "I think we managed to do that in the writing, and Michael Rymer, the actors and the crew all then brought a kinetic power to the scenes that knocked us out. The death of Socinus is perhaps the finest moment we have ever had the privilege of writing for the screen, thanks to Michael Rymer and the shattering performances by Aaron Douglas and all of the other actors in the scene."

Naturally, Socinus' tragic death proved to be one of the episode's most challenging and controversial moments. Another scene that provoked heavy debate among *Battlestar Galactica*'s makers was the dream sequence in which Baltar imagines Commander Adama drowning the Cylon-human baby.

"There was a lot of nervousness about whether we could show that," Moore reveals. "I thought it was a powerful way of setting up Baltar's interest in the baby and establishing that Adama will be an obstacle between Baltar and his destiny with regards to the child. In the end, we did get to do it but we didn't show that much. When we filmed it, we really went for it!"

Unsurprisingly, Edward James Olmos found the scene difficult to shoot. "It was a dream sequence, but it still was quite intense," he says. "What was interesting about it is that the Adama in season one would probably want to do that, but I'm not sure the Adama in season two would be so quick to do it."

As part of his final rewrite of 'Valley of Darkness', Moore added the scene in which Kara Thrace visits her former home on Caprica. Loosely inspired by earlier discussions about the possibility of Karl Agathon returning to his hometown in season one, the scene allowed the show to reveal more about Starbuck's life, back-story and personality.

"For me, that's the most groundbreaking scene in the episode," says Rymer. "You don't often see two people just hanging out for a moment, taking a break from the duress in a science fiction show. I don't think it's ever happened in a genre show."

"That's one of my favorite scenes of the entire series," Moore adds. "It's a great character scene and it's really moving and meaningful."

The scene features Bear McCreary's searing performance of Philip Glass' 1988 composition 'Metamorphosis Five'. "The original Philip Glass track was used on the rough cut of the episode and as soon as I saw it, I fell in love with it," Eick reveals. "So I went to great lengths to make a deal to use that specific cue."

With its blend of effects-packed action and touching character moments, 'Valley of Darkness' completed season two's opening two-part story-line in style. "I am extremely pleased with the way 'Scattered' and 'Valley of Darkness' came out," Weddle reports. "I am particularly proud of the sequences on Kobol."

"'Valley of Darkness' is a good episode," Moore concludes. "I think it turned out well. The great thing about it is that it carries the story forward in a way that makes it clear that season two is going places and is going to do things with the characters that season one could only hint at." ∎

SURVEILLANCE: ADDITIONAL

'Valley of Darkness' contains a brief dialogue exchange that held a lot of meaning for David Weddle. "I am thrilled that Commander Adama's expression 'Sometimes you gotta roll the hard six' was echoed by Lee in 'Valley of Darkness'," he reveals. "This is an expression my father used many times when I was growing up. It refers to a high stakes roll of the dice in [the American gambling game] craps. My father was saying that there are points in life where you have to take risks. If you don't, you will never achieve anything worthwhile."

Lee Adama's decision to roll a hard six was just the latest example of James O. Weddle's expression being used on the *Battlestar Galactica* sets. "During the making of season one, Brad and I were in Vancouver and we walked into the special effects department," Weddle continues. "There on the wall was a huge mock poster advertising the virtues of a Viper and the caption on the poster read: 'When you have to roll the hard six… Viper!' I have framed the poster and will be hanging it in our office."

[FRAGGED]

WRITERS: Dawn Prestwich & Nicole Yorkin
DIRECTOR: Sergio Mimica-Gezzan

GUEST CAST: Sam Witwer (Alex 'Crashdown' Quartararo), Kerry Norton (Paramedic Layne Ishay), Kurt Evans (Paramedic Howard Kim), Chris Shields (Corporal Venner), Jennifer Halley (Seelix), Patricia Idlette (Sarah Porter), Malcolm Stewart (Marshall Bagot)

"One of you will turn against the others..."
— Number Six, to Gaius Baltar

---

octor Cottle boards the *Galactica* to conduct an emergency operation on Commander Adama. With Adama's fate still looking uncertain, Colonel Tigh begins to drink heavily. When the Quorum of Twelve visit the *Galactica* demanding to see President Roslin, Tigh denies their request until his wife, Ellen, tells him that Roslin has lost her mind. But Roslin's odd behavior is actually a temporary symptom of her chamalla withdrawal and by the time she meets the other leaders, the President has regained her composure. Roslin calmly condemns Adama's recent actions and announces that she is the dying leader referred to in the Scrolls of Pythia and is destined to lead humankind to Earth.

Meanwhile, on Kobol, the surviving members of the survey team discover that the Cylons are constructing a missile battery that will wipe out everything in the area — as well as Captain Adama's search-and-rescue team. As the group prepare to launch an assault against the Cylons, Crashdown clashes with the other members of his team over his plan and aims his gun at Cally. But before he can fire, Crashdown is himself killed by Gaius Baltar. Under Chief Tyrol's command, the unit is then able to defeat the Cylons and destroy the missile battery's dradis, which allows Adama's raptor to rescue them. The group later tell Adama that Crashdown died heroically, in the line of duty.

Following the Quorum of Twelve's meeting with Roslin, Tigh decides he has no choice but to declare martial law...

Opposite: Gaius Baltar finds himself having to take drastic action.

SURVEILLANCE: ADDITIONAL

Paramedic Layne Ishay is played by British actress Kerry Norton. Best known for her role as Maxine Purvis in the UK TV series *Bad Girls*, Norton has also appeared in *EastEnders*, *Sabrina the Teenage Witch* and *Casualty*. Away from the cameras, Norton is the real-life wife of *Battlestar Galactica*'s 'Apollo', Jamie Bamber.

The resolution of Alex 'Crashdown' Quartararo's mission on Kobol was largely inspired by Sam Witwer's performance in the first-season finale, 'Kobol's Last Gleaming, Part II'. "The end of Crashdown was just a great story we really got into," explains Ronald D. Moore. "I don't think we set out to kill him at all when we put him down on Kobol at the end of season one. But his performance in 'Kobol's Last Gleaming' made us go, 'Wow, there's a great story here that will probably end in Crashdown's death,' because Sam portrayed this character who was clearly in over his head and yet was determined to do what he thought was right.

"Crashdown is clearly trying to do the right thing on Kobol," Moore continues. "He's

not an idiot, but he is inexperienced. He's not a ground officer. He's trying to be a leader and he's so committed to this idea of taking the Cylons out that he won't listen to anyone else. I think that gave us an interesting storyline and, as we developed 'Fragged', it was clear that the best ending of the story was killing him off."

When Sam Witwer learned of the producers' plans for Crashdown, he quickly embraced the dramatic potential of his character's last stand. "David Eick promised me a 'glorious death' and I really liked the sound of that," he reveals. "I also understood they already had a lot of characters from the miniseries to deal with, and I was anxious to get back to my music and some other pet projects in LA. So I was just flattered that they gave me such a wonderful opportunity to contribute dramatically to the show."

The task of killing Crashdown was assigned to the writing team of Dawn Prestwich and Nicole Yorkin, who scripted 'Fragged' following a series of story meetings with the show's writing staff. It was during those meetings that it was decided that Crashdown would be shot by none other than Gaius Baltar.

"We all agreed that season two should mark the rise of Gaius Baltar," explains Carla Robinson, "so while the Raptor crew was stranded on Kobol in season one, Baltar begins to make his move toward his destiny. How can Baltar stop what looks like a suicide mission? He can shoot first. I suggested that Baltar kill Crashdown. Baltar takes this action to conceal his continued perfidy and save his own life, but, in the process, he rescues the entire mission."

As the episode's script was finalized, Sergio Mimica-Gezzan was hired to direct 'Fragged'. Best known as the assistant director on such Steven Spielberg movies as *Schindler's List*, *Saving Private Ryan* and *The Terminal*, Mimica-Gezzan made his episodic television directing début with *Battlestar Galactica*'s acclaimed first season episode 'You Can't Go Home Again' and was a natural choice to helm the action-packed season two installment. Ironically, however, his appointment in the director's chair initially caused David Eick a moment of concern.

"When I first saw the script for 'Fragged' we didn't have a director," Eick explains, "and I was very excited about the opportunity to pay homage to the great moment in *Saving Private Ryan* where Tom Hanks is desperately shooting at the tank with his little handgun and suddenly, somehow, the tank blows up — because, we then find out, the Air Force has arrived and nailed it. It's a great Spielberg moment. So in doing the rewrite on that episode, I came up with the moment where Tyrol faces the Cylons and is saved by the Raptors.

"I was thrilled to book Sergio Mimica-Gezzan to direct the episode, because his first episode was really superb. But then I thought, 'Oh shit...', because Sergio was Spielberg's AD on *Saving Private Ryan* and I was worried he wouldn't want to

SURVEILLANCE: ADDITIONAL

'Fragged' was destined to be season two's only *Battlestar Galactica* episode scripted by Dawn Prestwich and Nicole Yorkin, as they left the show's writing staff shortly after completing it. "Essentially they found they did not like the genre as much as they thought they might," Moore reveals. "They had a little trouble with the show's combination of science fiction and military life; I don't think they were really interested in either. They liked the show, I liked them personally and they liked me, but they felt they wanted to do something else. So we let them go and that was all fine."

do the scene! But, fortunately for me, he thought it was a great homage and did it exactly as I hoped we would."

"That episode really was our *Saving Private Ryan*," agrees Aaron Douglas. "Sergio used the same kind of shots and gave it the same kind of feeling. It was thrilling to work on."

James Callis' most vivid memory of 'Fragged' concerns shooting Baltar's murder of Crashdown. "That was an amazing development for my character," he explains. "What's interesting about it is that it's the worst thing Baltar had done up to that point, and yet in a way it was the right thing to do.

Above: 'Fragged' represents a key episode for Baltar's character development in season two.

"It was a very emotional moment to shoot," he adds. "Luckily for me, Sam Witwer was very good about it. I saw him for lunch some time afterwards and he was very nice. He doesn't bear any grudges!"

"I was pleased to have my character's death contribute to Baltar's character development," says Witwer. "James Callis is just a great guy. If I had to go, I'd hoped it would be either him or Aaron Douglas pulling the trigger!"

While 'Fragged' primarily serves to conclude the survey team's fight for survival on Kobol, it also develops the civil war story arc by showing Colonel Tigh struggling to lead the *Galactica* and the fleet in peacetime. "Tigh is a man you want in command in a crisis/war-time situation," Moore notes. "He successfully guides everyone through 'Scattered' and 'Valley of Darkness'. But in 'Fragged', we start to see that when the crisis is over you really don't want Tigh in command, because he's not very political and he drinks too much."

Tigh's problems are worsened as President Roslin begins to use Colonial religious beliefs to increase her political support. "I thought it was really interesting for Laura to decide to play the religious card and call people to her banner in the name of their faith," says Moore of this storyline. "It raises some intriguing issues and character developments."

Ultimately, Moore feels that 'Fragged' provided an excellent continuation of the show's second season. "I was very happy with that episode," he states. "I thought it was one of our stronger offerings. I really enjoyed its Kobol storyline; I liked watching the disintegration of the unit stuck by themselves and I loved the final beat, with Crashdown pointing the gun at Cally, Tyrol pointing the gun at Crashdown and then Baltar shooting Crashdown. I thought that was a great moment. I also liked the bittersweet ending, with all of them lying to save Crashdown's reputation." ∎

[RESISTANCE]

WRITER: Toni Graphia
DIRECTOR: Allan Kroeker

GUEST CAST: Lorena Gale (Elosha), Tamara Lashley (Sue-Shaun), Jeremy Guilbaut (Lt Joe 'Hammerhead' Palladino), Chris Shields (Corporal Venner), Dominic Zamprogna (Jammer), Marine (Heather Doerksen)

"You shot people for throwing coffee?"
— Colonel Tigh, to Lieutenant Joe Palladino

Colonel Tigh's imposition of martial law divides both the *Galactica*'s crew and the civilian fleet, and results in several ships refusing to send Tylium fuel and other supplies to the *Galactica*. When Tigh dispatches military officers to enforce discipline on the supply ships, the officers panic in the face of heated civil unrest and open fire, killing four civilians.

Appalled by the disaster, President Roslin and Captain Lee Adama decide they must break out of prison to establish a democratic opposition. With the help of various people including Corporal Venner, Dr Cottle, Dualla and Tom Zarek, they make a successful break for freedom just before Commander Adama regains consciousness.

As the political drama escalates, Tyrol finds himself accused of being a Cylon and is imprisoned with Sharon 'Boomer' Valerii. Cally blames Sharon for Tyrol's predicament and decides she has no choice but to assassinate the Cylon, who dies in Tyrol's arms.

Far away from the fleet, on Cylon-occupied Caprica, Kara Thrace and Karl Agathon encounter a group of fifty-three humans who survived the nuclear holocaust because they were in the mountains. These humans include Samuel T. Anders, a former professional pyramid player who Kara quickly forms a close bond with...

SURVEILLANCE: ADDITIONAL

An early draft of the script for 'Resistance' had Ellen Tigh in CIC encouraging her husband to shoot down President Roslin and Lee Adama's ship as they escape the *Galactica*. The producers also planned for Boomer to refer to Chief Tyrol by his first name, Galen, during her dying moments, but decided against the idea. "Tyrol's first name tends to get a chuckle the first time people hear it," explains Moore, "and I didn't want that spoiling the moment for the audience."

'Resistance' began life as a card on the wall of the writers' room in *Battlestar Galactica*'s Los Angeles production office. The card simply had two words written on it: 'Kent State'. "The idea was for us to do an episode in which the military clashed with civilians, à la 'Kent State'," explains 'Resistance' writer Toni Graphia, referring to the notorious 1970 incident in which the US National Guard shot and killed four anti-war protestors during a heated rally at the Kent State University campus. "We wanted to explore what it would be like if tensions were running high and the military overstepped its bounds in some frenzy and innocent civilians were killed.

"We combined the idea with a much earlier idea Ron had," she continues. "Ron always wanted to do a whole episode called just 'Paper'. It was simply going to be about what happened if the fleet ran out of paper. We talked about that and asked

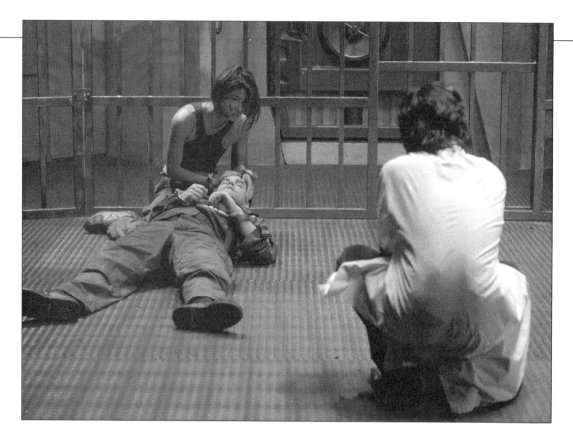

ourselves, 'What could we run out of that would make everyone go nuts?' Being writers we naturally came up with coffee! So we put those things together in the episode."

"As the show developed, we increasingly moved away from the Kent State reference," adds Ronald D. Moore. "Ultimately, what happens in the episode has more in common with the Boston Massacre, where a group of British Redcoats were backed up against a building in Boston by a mob and the situation got out of control and somebody stared firing."

In keeping with its title, Graphia's script also served to establish Laura Roslin's break for freedom as part of the show's ongoing story arc and revealed the existence of a human resistance movement on Cylon-occupied Caprica. "It was Ron's idea that the resistance fighters would be a professional Pyramid team that had been training up in the mountains," she reveals. "I thought that was just brilliant, especially because it helped set up the romance between Anders and Kara, since the Series Bible established that she had played Pyramid.

"We had a lot of fun developing the idea of the resistance," adds Graphia with a smile. "Our real-world parallel was, 'What if Los Angeles was destroyed and then the LA Lakers came down out of the mountains, took up guns and went on a rampage?' That was the image we were working with that made it vivid and real to us."

While writing 'Resistance', one of Graphia's key additions to the script was the surprise death of Sharon 'Boomer' Valerii. The character was originally supposed to survive her walk through the *Galactica* to her newly-constructed cage prison and was set to become the subject of various experiments in the show's following episodes.

"As I was writing, I got a new idea," Graphia recalls. "Ron and I both share a fascination with the JFK conspiracy and have many books on the subject. When he wrote the season one finale ['Kobol's Last Gleaming, Part I'], he compared Adama being shot and the chaos that followed with how it must have been in the moments following the Kennedy assassination. So I came up with the idea that if Boomer was essentially our Lee Harvey Oswald, what if we had a Jack Ruby who, in turn, shot her? Our natural Jack Ruby was Cally. She loved Adama, idolized Tyrol and felt betrayed by Boomer."

On deciding she wanted to kill off Boomer, Graphia asked the show's other writers for their opinions. "They all loved it and said, 'Go for it! But don't tell Ron — let it be a surprise and then you'll really know if it works or not.' So I went ahead and wrote it, and then just held my breath!

"It was a big risk, because Ron could have hated it. Luckily, he read it and loved it. I had a feeling he would, especially because of the JFK parallels."

Graphia's 'risky' idea also won the approval of Cally's real-life alter ego, Nicki Clyne. "I was shocked when I first read that script," she admits, "but it was also very exciting that they were willing to give my character such an important role. I thought it made perfect sense for Cally to kill Boomer, because of her feelings for Tyrol and the trauma she had been through."

The task of bringing Boomer's death to the screen was allocated to Allan Kroeker, a veteran television director who had previously helmed the first season *Battlestar Galactica* installment 'Bastille Day' (also scripted by Graphia). Kroeker sought to base Sharon's demise on Jack Ruby's murder of Lee Harvey Oswald. "We were all told they wanted to mimic the Oswald assassination," Grace Park confirms. "I looked at photos of the assassination and rented some movies like *JFK*."

In addition to delivering the demise of Boomer, 'Resistance' sees Baltar continuing to emerge as a darker and more dangerous presence on the *Galactica*. It also provides further evidence of Colonel Tigh's limitations as a commanding officer during peacetime. "We really put Tigh in an unfavorable light in 'Resistance'," Eick notes. "As the episode opens, he's beating the shit out of Chief Tyrol, who's one of the audience's favorite characters. And it just gets worse from there. But the wonderful thing about Michael Hogan is that there's something about his performance and its completely uncompromising nature that still makes him a very sympathetic character, despite everything."

Tigh's actions in 'Resistance' provoke Laura Roslin to mount an escape bid with her trusted allies. These allies were initially set to include Billy Keikeya, until concerns about the actor's availability forced Moore to leave him on the *Galactica*. "We didn't know if Paul would be available for the next few episodes," Moore recalls, "so we

SURVEILLANCE: ADDITIONAL

Although it takes its name from the card game featured in the original *Battlestar Galactica*, Pyramid was loosely inspired by another of the original series' games, Triad. A full-contact sport, Pyramid is played on a triangular court that contains a goal in one corner. The object of the game is to place the ball in the goal as many times as possible. Pyramid is played by two teams, which can consist of one, three or five players. Players cannot step more than three paces without passing the ball, shooting at the goal or bouncing the ball off a wall.

temporarily wrote him out."

The latter part of 'Resistance' also establishes the attraction between Kara and Anders via their game of Pyramid. Originally scripted to take place in a racquetball-type court, Pyramid became an outside, basketball-style game due to budgetary factors. Pyramid's basic rules were shaped by the show's producers and then developed by Kroeker, stunt coordinator Mike Mitchell and assistant stunt coordinator Duane Dickinson. "We were told about the rules and then just told to go for it," explains Katee Sackhoff. "It was a lot of fun.

"I loved shooting that stuff with Michael Trucco," she continues. "We played for something like five hours. We practiced for an hour before we started shooting and we only scored about three goals between us in that hour; it's hard to score goals in that game, because the goal is so small. But when we actually started shooting, I scored on the first shot! That was great.

"Unfortunately," she admits with a grin, "I didn't score again after that."

'Resistance' concludes with Commander Adama awakening from his coma and preparing to face the aftermath of both his and Tigh's recent actions. "I think at this point, the audience is ready for Adama to get back into the show," says Moore. "The way we play it, it's a nice surprise for the audience. And the great thing is that Eddie's performance reminds you Adama's been hurt; it's not the usual 'miracle recovery' you see on TV." ■

Above: Kara Thrace and Samuel T Anders play Pyramid.

[THE FARM]

WRITER: Carla Robinson
DIRECTOR: Rod Hardy

GUEST CAST: Rick Worthy (Simon), Lorena Gale (Elosha),
Tamara Lashley (Sue-Shaun)

"Lords of Kobol, please help me..." — Lieutenant Kara Thrace

Kara Thrace is wounded in a surprise Cylon attack on the Caprica resistance and knocked unconscious. She awakens in a converted medical facility to find herself being nursed back to health by Simon, an attentive doctor who claims to be part of the resistance. Simon also tells Kara about her need to reproduce and questions her about physical evidence of the abuse she received as a child.

When Kara awakens to discover she has been operated on again, she secretly investigates the facility and discovers that the hospital is actually run by Cylons. After she kills Simon, she tries to leave the facility and discovers a room full of women who are wired to Cylon breeding machinery. Kara destroys the machinery and is then rescued from the Cylon breeding farm by the resistance, led by Samuel Anders and Karl Agathon. The mission is aided by Sharon Valerii, who joins them with a Cylon Heavy Raider.

Following their escape, Kara, Sharon and Helo leave Caprica to return to Kobol. But before they depart, Kara promises Anders she will return for him one day.

Back on the *Galactica*, Commander Adama's first task on returning to duty is to track down President Roslin and her allies. As Adama orders every ship in the fleet to be searched, Roslin broadcasts a message. She announces herself as the voice of the prophet Pythia and asks the fleet's population to return with her to Kobol. Adama doesn't believe anyone will join Roslin, but is shocked when a third of the fleet follow her...

SURVEILLANCE: ADDITIONAL

Simon is able to refer to Samuel Anders while interacting with Kara Thrace because the Cylons had been tracking Anders' work with the Caprica resistance. The show's producers considered revealing that Anders' cell had been infiltrated by a Cylon agent, but the concept never made it into the episode's script.

'The Farm' represents the first *Battlestar Galactica* episode to follow a primary plotline set on Cylon-occupied Caprica. Its premise was conceived in a writers' meeting early in the development of season two and provided the series with an opportunity to reveal more about Kara Thrace and the Cylons' activities on Caprica.

"The A-plot didn't really change that much from start to finish," Moore recalls. "The only real difference was that Kara was originally going to be aware that she was in a Cylon facility from the start, which we changed so that we could introduce an element of mystery. We also originally talked about Kara freeing everyone from the facility at the end.

"'The Farm' was one of the most controversial episodes of the season," he reveals. "It was a dark story and there were concerns it would scare off female viewers,

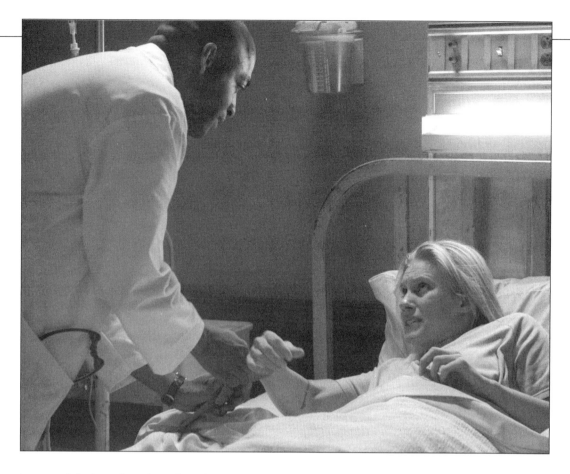

Above: Kara Thrace finds herself at the mercy of the Cylons.

because of the issues it explores about female reproductive organs. But we fought to do it and I think it turned out well."

Initial script duties on 'The Farm' were assigned to staff writer Carla Robinson, who had previously penned the first season Starbuck showcase 'You Can't Go Home Again' as well as the later season one installment 'Colonial Day'. "I felt very liberated in writing this episode," says Robinson. "Ron Moore and David Eick issued me a license to be as creepy as I wanted to be, so I really went for it! I wanted to put Starbuck, a fierce character, in a truly vulnerable position.

"I so enjoyed writing the episode, examining various ways an injured, medicated, near-naked woman could break out of an enemy facility. I'm so glad I had Starbuck to work with!"

As Kara fights to escape the Cylon facility, viewers learn details of Kara Thrace's childhood abuse by her mother. This element of Kara's back-story had been established by Moore's Series Bible and had previously been hinted at throughout the series. "Each draft of the script delved more deeply into Starbuck's painful childhood," Robinson recalls. "In the produced version, she breaks emotionally as she faces the personal abuse she has tried to repress. But she's still Starbuck, and she realizes that Simon has played her like a violin, forcing her to relive her past."

Veteran TV guest star Rick Worthy (*Murder One, Star Trek: Enterprise*) was cast as Kara's nemesis in the episode, while Rod Hardy was invited to direct following his work on the season one installments 'Act of Contrition' and 'Litmus'. "We were lucky to get Rod Hardy for that episode," says David Eick, "because it was a performance piece that dealt with Hitchcockian tension. It was an episode that could have gone wrong on a number of fronts, but with Rod and Katee Sackhoff at the center it became one of the most powerful episodes we'd done."

Sackhoff herself welcomed the rich dramatic opportunities presented by 'The Farm'. "That was a really interesting episode for me," she explains. "It answered a lot of questions about what had happened to Starbuck and why she is the way she is. It shows that she's been scarred by the abuse she suffered as a child and her relationship with her mother.

"I was shocked when I first heard about all that," Sackhoff reveals. "But I thought it was a brave move on the part of the writers and it explains a lot about Kara's relationship with President Roslin. I had been asking why Kara seemed guarded around the President and I guess she has a problem with women in positions of power over her."

One of the episode's most unusual moments for Sackhoff involved the shooting of Simon's gynecological examination of Kara. The concept of the examination was first suggested by Robinson, who saw it as a way of highlighting Kara's vulnerability. "When I found out I'd be having a pelvic exam I had a heart attack," Sackhoff recalls. "I was like, 'That's not fun in real life. I don't want to fake it on camera!'

"It was funny really," she adds. "I had just met the actor and then my legs were spread in a very compromising position. I was just sitting there going, 'This is so bad!'"

"That scene was extremely controversial," adds Moore. "There were concerns about it being too distasteful. But I felt it wasn't anything you don't see on medical dramas like *ER*, so I argued for it to be kept in the episode."

While Kara's hospital room was actually a set in Vancouver Film Studios, other scenes based in the Cylon facility were shot on location at Vancouver's Riverview Hospital. "'The Farm' was a fun episode for us," says Richard Hudolin. "It required us to intermingle what the Cylons would have for a hospital and what humans would understand a hospital to be. We wanted to give the hospital an ominous and almost gothic feeling.

"The Cylon experimentation room was something we built on location. It combines Cylon technology with Colonial stuff. I had to cut back a lot of my ideas for it due to budgetary reasons, but I think it works."

Following her escape from the facility, Kara leaves Caprica for the *Galactica*. But before she does so, she promises Anders she will return for him, in a moment that sets the scene for later episodes. She also learns more about the Cylons' inability to

SURVEILLANCE: ADDITIONAL

When Kara is shot in the episode's teaser, her wound changes side. This was done deliberately, to reflect Kara's confusion as she loses consciousness.

reproduce and their grand plan of creating Cylon-human hybrids, thanks to Sharon Valerii.

"The finished episode gives us a peek into Cylon culture and the Cylon plan," Robinson points out. "We suggest in this episode that despite the Cylon belief of superiority over the human race, they may need humans after all to ensure their own survival."

The close of the Caprica storyline deliberately leaves viewers wondering what the Cylons did to Kara. "That was something we always planned to come back to," explains Moore. "We've always said that the Cylons believe Kara is special and has a destiny. We reveal the Cylons have taken some of Kara's ovaries, but we wanted to leave you wondering what they are going to do with them."

The B-plot of 'The Farm' develops the civil war story arc, as President Roslin broadcasts a message that leads the fleet to split into two factions. This episode begins with Roslin, Lee Adama and Elosha hiding in a "freezer room" aboard the *Kimba Hutu* — which was actually a set built on location at Riverview Hospital. "They were originally going to be hiding in a meat locker," Hudolin recalls, "but it was going to be too hard for us to put a film unit into an actual meat locker or freezer. So I came up with the idea of doing the freezer room. We created it out of wax and stuff like that and I think it looks fairly effective."

Above: The final moments of 'The Farm' see Commander Adama finally back on his feet.

'The Farm' also features Commander Adama's long-awaited return to duty. "Adama's return to command was something we talked about at length," says Moore. "We knew he'd be affected by the shooting, so he comes back a changed man. His emotions are nearer the surface and he's philosophical about things. We knew that would be interesting to explore and that it would have interesting repercussions as the show continued." ∎

[HOME, PART I]

WRITER: David Eick
DIRECTOR: Sergio Mimica-Gezzan

GUEST CAST: James Remar (Meier), Patricia Idlette (Sarah Porter), Malcolm Stewart (Marshall Bagot), Ben Ayres (Lt George 'Catman' Birch), Linnea Sharples (Lt Emmitt 'Sweetness' Jones), Christina Schild (Playa), Biski Gugushe (Sekou Hamilton), Raahul Singh (Kimmitt)

"I'm putting the fleet back together. I'm putting our family back together. This ends now." — Commander William Adama

Kara Thrace and Karl Agathon join the rebel fleet and immediately find themselves having to protect Sharon Valerii. President Roslin orders the Cylon's death, but her execution is cancelled after Sharon tells Roslin she can help her find the Tomb of Athena on Kobol.

Back on the *Galactica*, Commander Adama and Colonel Tigh attempt to adjust to life without a third of the fleet and appoint Lieutenant George Birch as the *Galactica*'s new CAG. But Birch is clearly too inexperienced for the assignment and struggles in his new role. Following an uncomfortable exchange with Anastasia Dualla about his broken promise to find Earth, Adama realizes he must reunite the fleet and orders the *Galactica* to set course for Kobol.

Meanwhile, on Kobol, Roslin's landing party sets off in search of the Tomb of Athena. After Elosha is killed by a Cylon trap, Sharon helps save the group from a Centurion attack. But as they continue on their quest, Tom Zarek's companion Meier plots to aid his friend's rise to power…

SURVEILLANCE: ADDITIONAL

The scene in which Baltar tells Number Six about his new perspective on humankind was added to 'Home, Part I' when the producers realized the characters would otherwise be completely absent from the episode. Written by Ronald D. Moore, the scene was loosely inspired by his last trip to Alaska, where Moore visited salmon spawning areas. "I liked that scene," says David Eick. "It's creepy yet kind of sexy."

"'Home' is essentially the end of season one," says Ronald D. Moore of the epic two-part adventure. "It resolves all the arcs from season one and the season finale, 'Kobol's Last Gleaming'. After 'Home', we open up new arcs and, in a way, really begin season two."

The task of scripting the resolution to the power struggle between Commander Adama and President Roslin was tackled by David Eick, who was also responsible for developing the storyline for 'Kobol's Last Gleaming' and the subsequent civil war story arc with Moore. While Eick had played a major role in shaping *Battlestar Galactica*'s scripts and storylines from the beginning of the show, 'Home' marked his first foray into penning the first draft of a script for the series.

"I'd always wanted to take a crack at writing an episode," Eick reveals. "I'd had a really nice experience working the story out for the season one finale and Ron had been very encouraging about it. But I think I drew the short straw with 'Home', because when you're writing your first episodic teleplay, the last thing you want is to have to wrap up everything from the past eighteen episodes! It was quite an ordeal. But I took it really

seriously and I enjoyed it."

Eick entitled his script 'Home' to reflect the idea that it reunited all the show's main characters and brought them all back to the *Galactica*. He quickly secured one of his favorite directors on the show, Sergio Mimica-Gezzan, to bring his script to the screen. "When we were shooting 'Fragged', I made Sergio promise me we wouldn't do anything that wasn't great," Eick recalls. "It was my first episode as a writer, so I really wanted it to be special."

'Home' was originally conceived and written as a single episode. But with so many plot points and character developments to address, Eick's first draft of the script was sixty-five pages in length — some fifteen pages longer than a standard *Battlestar Galactica* script.

"Writing the episode proved such an immense task that it wasn't until I'd spent about a month on the first draft that I looked at it and realized we had too much for one episode," Eick explains. "We had enough material for one and a half episodes. So at a very late stage, about a week before we started prep on the episode, we called the network and the studio and asked to expand it into a two-parter. Fortunately, they agreed. It

(HOME, PART I)

Above: Tom Zarek's true motives remain a mystery.

was a brave move because the original script was extremely character-driven and didn't have a plot engine that lent itself to being a two-parter like 'Act of Contrition' and 'You Can't Go Home Again' did. So Acts I and II of my original script essentially became 'Home, Part I'."

'Home, Part I' begins with President Roslin's rebel fleet heading to Kobol and being joined by Kara Thrace, Karl Agathon and the pregnant Sharon Valerii. Their return from Caprica provides the basis of some great drama as well as a memorable reunion between Kara and Lee Adama, a key element of which was prompted by a suggestion from Jamie Bamber.

"I told David Eick that Lee should kiss Kara," Bamber recalls. "I thought that was a natural response for the character and it was a great moment. I also loved the way the scene immediately shifts into a very powerful confrontation between my character, Helo and Sharon."

Once Roslin's group returns to Kobol, the mythology of the show called for a key member of her team to lose their life during the mission. While continued concerns over

Paul Campbell's availability to work on the series meant that Billy Keikeya was quickly earmarked as a possible fatality, the character was ultimately spared on this occasion. Elosha, however, was less fortunate and became a victim of a Kobol mine inspired by World War II's 'bouncing betties'.

"It was necessary for someone to die on Kobol because we'd always talked about there being a cost in blood," Eick notes. "And because Roslin's role as a prophet was drawing to a close, it seemed right that we killed the person who guided her to that point."

"Before we decided to kill her off, we did have other plans for Elosha," Moore adds. "We planned to show her really stepping to the fore later on in the season and pushing her own agenda by manipulating Laura to pass certain laws."

While Laura's team fights for their lives, Commander Adama tries to cope with the loss of a third of the fleet's population. Adama's struggle is highlighted by his selection of a new CAG, George Birch, who was named after Eick's father-in-law James Birchfield.

"The plotline about Adama trying to find a new CAG went through a lot of internal strife," Moore reveals. "It's an unusual storyline, in that it's not about a crisis or a matter of life and death. It was initially going to be more dramatic in that people were going to get killed as a result of the failed refueling mission, but we decided against doing that because it would have made Adama look really stupid to choose Birch."

The failure of the refueling mission was originally conceived as the incident that inspires Adama to return to Kobol and reunite the fleet. During the production of the episode, however, it was decided that Adama's emotional exchange with Dualla would be the turning point instead, and the positioning of the two sequences was swapped.

"I thought that was an interesting thing to do," says Moore of the Adama/Dualla confrontation. "We'd been playing with the idea that Dualla is a special person in the family. She's the person everyone communicates through and with, so there's a certain trust and intimacy people have with her. People listen to her, even if her opinions are not always elicited. And I liked the idea of her refusing to stop until she's said her piece."

"That was a really powerful scene for me," adds Kandyse McClure. "I was surprised by how Dualla was able to buck authority for a moment to express herself and I liked that she wasn't angry with Adama, but just disappointed with him, because she believes in him. I was really grateful to David Eick and Ron Moore for giving me the opportunity to really flex my acting muscles a bit."

At Eick's suggestion, the moment in which Adama realizes the time has come to reunite the fleet was accompanied by the return of an uplifting musical cue from season one's 'The Hand of God'. The scene brings the episode to a moving close.

"I thought Sergio did a great job with 'Home, Part I'," states Eick. "Ron had warned me that an episode never comes out the way a writer expects, but I thought very little changed and I was very pleased with how Sergio handed it. I think we were able to make a very good episode." ∎

[HOME, PART II]

WRITERS: David Eick &
Ronald D. Moore
DIRECTOR: Jeff Woolnough

GUEST CAST: James Remar (Meier)

"This is the map... This is the map to Earth." — Captain Adama

President Laura Roslin's landing party continues its difficult trek across Kobol in search of the Tomb of Athena. With tension mounting between Tom Zarek and Lee Adama, Zarek's old friend Meier plans to move against Adama and his allies in an attempt to clear Zarek's path to power.

Back on the *Galactica*, Commander Adama announces that he will personally lead the Raptor mission to Kobol. Accompanied by Billy Keikeya, Adama successfully locates Roslin's group and forges peace with her. When Meier later attempts to move against the group before they can enter the Tomb of Athena, he is thwarted by Sharon Valerii. Following the incident, Adama joins Roslin, Lee, Billy and Kara Thrace inside the Tomb of Athena, where they use the Arrow of Apollo to access a map of the long route to Earth.

Returning to the *Galactica*, Commander Adama publicly restores Laura Roslin as President of the Twelve Colonies of Kobol and the fleet is reunited. Meanwhile, Gaius Baltar finds himself questioning his sanity after Number Six tells him there is no Cylon computer chip inside his brain...

When 'Home' became a two-part adventure, David Eick and Ronald D. Moore immediately went to dinner to discuss what they needed to add to make the two episodes work. "We essentially had a script for an episode and a half and had to come up with more material," explains Eick, who co-wrote 'Home, Part II' with Moore. "The second half of 'Part II' is essentially the second half of the original episode, but the first half is material we added."

Opposite: Sharon Valerii finds herself embroiled in a deadly plot.

One of the additions to 'Home, Part II' was the subplot in which Number Six tells Baltar that she is purely a figment of his imagination, rather than the product of a Cylon computer chip. "That was a storyline we had talked about doing in season one," Moore recalls. "I loved the idea and had always wanted to do it, and it went in and out of a couple of episodes. So when 'Home' became two episodes, we decided to explore this storyline. It's a fun plotline and James Callis is wonderful in it."

'Home, Part II' was helmed by another of Eick's favorite *Battlestar Galactica* directors, Jeff Woolnough. Woolnough had previously directed the excellent first season episode 'The Hand of God'. "It was a uniquely difficult episode to make," Eick notes, "because

SURVEILLANCE: ADDITIONAL

The scene in which Number Six sits naked in front of Baltar with only the rear of her chair to protect her modesty was inspired by the 1989 movie *Scandal*.

it involved all the characters and a lot of location work. We also wanted scenes to take place in the rain, which is a great way to make things more dramatic and visually interesting, but generally isn't easy to do."

'Home, Part II' begins with a teaser that intercuts scenes on the *Galactica* with events on Kobol, in a style reminiscent of the season one episode that began the Kobol story arc, 'Kobol's Last Gleaming, Part I'. The similarity between the two teasers is underlined by Bear McCreary's score. "Like 'Kobol's Last Gleaming, Part I', which began with a piece called 'Passacaglia', 'Home, Part II' begins with a five-minute montage score with string orchestra," McCreary explains. "This new piece quotes the theme from 'Passacaglia' and is used to suggest the end of the entire nine-episode Kobol story arc."

Following its teaser, 'Home, Part II' sees Commander Adama taking a Raptor to Kobol. The Raptor landing sequence was shot using a high-pressure air blaster to suggest the presence of strong G-forces. It also originally featured two lines that were changed on the orders of the Federal Communications Commission, to adhere to its broadcasting standards. "We weren't allowed to use Tyrol's line 'typography is for pussies' or Adama's joke, 'Adar was a prick'," Moore recalls. "It was very annoying."

Once on the planet's surface, Adama shares an emotional reunion with his son, Lee, in a scene Jamie Bamber enjoyed because of its "non-verbal" nature. Adama then forges an understanding with Roslin. "That scene establishes a new dynamic between Adama and Roslin, who were at odds from the start of the show," Moore notes. "We see them starting to call each other by their first names."

The scene also sees Adama telling Laura he forgives her for sparking the rebellion, and Laura responding by saying that she doesn't need his forgiveness. "I loved that moment, but it was very controversial with some of our male directors," Mary McDonnell reveals. "Michael Rymer said to me, 'Why doesn't Laura just say thank you?' But I thought it was important to show that Laura doesn't need Adama's validation. Instead, she's essentially saying to him, 'I'm glad you've finally resolved this drama of your own making for yourself.'"

The original draft of 'Home' lacked a confrontation between Adama and Sharon on Kobol. This was added after Edward James Olmos told David Eick he was looking forward to facing Sharon in the episode, because he felt Adama would stop at nothing to kill Sharon if he saw her again. Sharon's line to Adama, "And you ask why?" was later added by Moore, who felt it lent an "interesting sense of mystery" to the scene.

After narrowly surviving her first encounter with Adama, Sharon prevents the assassination plot that Meier has been hatching since the opening part of 'Home'. The show's producers were thrilled that Zarek's doomed henchman was played by veteran film actor James Remar, whose credits include *The Warriors* and *48 Hrs*. "David and I were big fans of James Remar's work and were excited to get him," says Moore. "He's a great bad guy for us in 'Home'."

The closing section of 'Home, Part II' sees Adama and Roslin entering the Tomb of Athena and discovering details of the route to Earth. The mythological elements of this

sequence were inspired by real-world classical myths and were the subject of extensive research conducted by James Halpern.

"We reveal a lot of the mythos of the show in this episode," Moore notes. "We outline a lot of things we had talked about in the writers' room, but had never revealed. We also connect everything to our present-day zodiac as well as the Greek and Roman myths."

The presentation of the map to Earth was the subject of detailed debate among the show's makers. In the original script, a vision of the constellations was briefly projected above the group before the Cylons mounted a new attack. But the idea was reworked when Gary Hutzel suggested that the group should "be in Stonehenge", while plans for the Cylon attack were abandoned. "There was a lot of back and forth on this internally," Moore confirms. "Ultimately we decided to go with the cleanest and best way of communicating the idea to the audience."

'Home, Part II' concludes with Adama reasserting Roslin's position as President of the Twelve Colonies of Kobol, in a scene inspired by the 1980 film *Brubaker*. "I got Jeff to watch *Brubaker* a few days before we started shooting and he did a fairly faithful lift from the end of the film," Eick notes. "I think it's a very moving end to the episode." ■

[FINAL CUT]

WRITER: Mark Verheiden
DIRECTOR: Robert Young

GUEST CAST: Lucy Lawless (D'Anna Biers), Matthew Bennett (Doral), Flick Harrison (Bell), Ty Olsson (Captain Aaron Kelly), Jeremy Guilbaut (Lt Joe 'Hammerhead' Palladino), Kevan Kase (Private Scott Kelso)

> "I want to show the people what life aboard the *Galactica* is really like. I want to put a human face on the officers and the crew..."
> — **President Laura Roslin, to D'Anna Biers**

When reporter D'Anna Biers acquires footage of military officers opening fire on civilian protestors aboard the *Gideon* during Colonel Tigh's command of the fleet, she is invited to meet Commander Adama and President Roslin. Intent on improving relations between the civilian fleet and the military, Roslin and Adama suggest Biers should make a report about life on the *Galactica* and promise her unlimited access to the Battlestar's crew.

As her report takes shape, Biers learns that Colonel Tigh has received a death threat and later identifies Tigh's would-be murderer as Lieutenant Palladino, the officer in charge of the troops who opened fire on the *Gideon*. Biers also witnesses Lieutenant Louanne 'Kat' Katraine crash-landing on the *Galactica* as a result of her over-use of stims and catches a glimpse of Dr Cottle saving the life of Sharon's unborn baby.

Armed with these explosive secrets, Biers ultimately produces a fairly balanced report that Adama gives his approval to. The report, and the rest of Biers' unscreened footage, is later viewed by a group of Cylons on Cylon-occupied Caprica. This group includes another model of Biers, who is also known as Number Three...

Devised as season two's first stand-alone installment, 'Final Cut' was inspired by discussions in the writers' room about the idea of making an episode from the perspective of a reporter aboard the *Galactica* and the possibility of depicting on-screen interviews with the show's characters. After considering various options, Ronald D. Moore and David Eick settled on the concept of an episode that followed a reporter making a documentary about life on the *Galactica*. This premise was then assigned to first-time *Battlestar Galactica* scriptwriter Mark Verheiden.

"Ron and David wanted to do a stand-alone, day-in-the-life type show that explored some of the less featured characters and gave the world of the ship some additional texture," Verheiden recalls. "I had just joined the show when this episode came up so it was my baptism of fire, and it was a fun way to start because it was all about exploring the characters.

"My personal mandate was to surprise the viewer — and Ron and David — with

SURVEILLANCE: ADDITIONAL

D'Anna Biers was named after David Eick's best friend in college, Joey D'Anna. "I was able to annoy him a little bit by making him a Cylon," Eick reveals with a chuckle.

Above: D'Anna Biers quizzes William Adama during the making of her behind-the-scenes look at life on *Galactica*.

unexpected character beats while maintaining the semi-documentary feel," he reveals. "As we dug into the story, we also thought it was important to show how the months of never-ending combat were wearing on the pilots and crew of *Galactica*, hence the story-line about Kat's addiction to stimulants. My favorite beats, though, were Gaeta revealing his fresh tattoo — which was originally going to be on his butt — and a deleted scene that shows Tyrol stapling together tattered uniforms because they're running out of thread and you don't want to use staples on your torn underwear.

"For anyone who wonders where these crazy ideas come from," Verheiden adds with a chuckle, "I actually knew a guy who would staple torn seams in his pants because he couldn't sew!"

While 'Final Cut' is driven by the making of D'Anna Biers' documentary, the episode also contains a subplot concerning a death threat to Colonel Tigh. "We felt the story needed some sort of jeopardy and decided to show the ramifications of the violent 'coffee rebellion' [in 'Resistance'] on Lieutenant Palladino and Colonel Tigh," explains Verheiden. "'Final Cut' originally ended with Palladino killing himself in Tigh's quarters, but it was eventually decided that a suicide was too dark and the scene became the talk-down that you see in the episode."

Early in the episode's development, Eick earmarked the role of D'Anna Biers for Lucy Lawless, his former colleague on *Xena: Warrior Princess*. Lawless had previously passed on the opportunity to play other characters in the series — including the role of Ellen Tigh — but was instantly engaged by the idea of playing a reporter with a big secret.

"I thought it was a very intriguing role," says Lawless. "I liked the duality of it; the mix of light and shade always appeals to me. All of my favorite characters are on a moral precipice."

"The great thing about casting Lucy in this role was that we could use her without undermining the reality we had created on the show," Eick adds. "I had seen Lucy just before we cast her and I knew she looked very different than she did on *Xena*, especially with her blonde hair. I also knew she had a substantial Kiwi accent in real life that she covered when she did *Xena* by doing an American accent. So I thought we could bring Lucy into the show without taking viewers out of the show. It was a win-win situation."

D'Anna Biers was initially described as a serious and determined journalist, and was loosely modeled on real-life CNN reporter Christiana Amanpour. "Christiana Amanpour was partly an inspiration for me in this role," Lawless confirms. "I saw D'Anna as a very driven reporter, with very rational motives."

The task of bringing 'Final Cut' to the screen was given to award-winning documentary maker Robert Young. Young had previously directed the first season *Battlestar Galactica* episode 'Six Degrees of Separation' and his return to the show was warmly welcomed by its cast and crew.

"It felt like a natural fit to have Robert do this episode," says Moore. "I felt that it was important to give the director, writer and actors a lot of space to improvise and to really embroider on the characters and on life on *Galactica*."

"Robert Young is one of my heroes," Lawless adds. "He's a legend. I was well aware of his work and have seen a lot of his films and documentaries, although I didn't know he was going to be directing the episode when I was up for the job. It was just fantastic to work with him."

Young's work on 'Final Cut' included the task of shooting D'Anna Biers' interviews with key *Galactica* officers. This gave Lawless a welcome opportunity to interact with the bulk of the show's regular cast.

"The interviews were such a pleasure to do," says Lawless. "They were all wonderful to shoot and they were also all very different. For example, the scenes between D'Anna Biers and Commander Adama were very complex; I played it as if she had the hots for him a little bit, as the alpha male. D'Anna's interaction with Starbuck is at the other extreme; there's a real sense of antagonism between them. There was just a terrific variety there."

Several scenes of 'Final Cut' show Lawless and her co-star, Flick Harrison, using genuine camera equipment. Much of their footage actually made it into the finished episode. "Flick Harrison was hired to play D'Anna's cameraman because he's a video cameraman as well as an actor, so we always planned to use some of his DV cam footage," Stephen McNutt reveals. "But, ultimately, Lucy did a lot of it herself. She really got into using the equipment and she had a great time with it."

SURVEILLANCE: ADDITIONAL

The acronyms featured in D'Anna Biers' documentary include CF (Colonial Fleet), CFR (Colonial Fleet Reserve), CMC (Colonial Marine Corps) and CMCR (Colonial Marine Corps Reserve).

Above: Colonel Tigh is forced to face the aftermath of the 'Gideon massacre'.

Among many other things, D'Anna Biers' documentary reveals the first names of Lieutenant Gaeta and Petty Officer Dualla. The characters were called Felix and Anastasia respectively by Moore, following his Internet search of ancient and classical names. At Moore's suggestion, the documentary footage also employs the 'clipped corners' design motif seen on the show's books, documents and pictures, which helps distinguish the documentary from the actual episode. The documentary footage is accompanied by a narration written by Moore.

"I wanted to outline the thesis of the show," he explains. "There's a nobility and heroism to these people. Despite their flaws and their dysfunction and their mistakes, these people are the guardians of the fleet — and that's the thing that makes them special."

Biers' documentary also memorably employs the original *Battlestar Galactica*'s theme tune, in what Moore describes as an affectionate nod to the franchise's past. The original theme tune was re-arranged and re-orchestrated by Bear McCreary, with the help of original composer Stu Phillips. "The finished product was a combination of traditional orchestral writing from the original *Battlestar* and ethnic soloists and percussion from the new *Battlestar*," McCreary reveals.

'Final Cut' ends with the revelation that D'Anna Biers is a Cylon. Shot in an actual cinema in Vancouver, the closing scene proved to be one of the episode's obvious highlights for Moore. "I think it's a great ending," he states. "We never hint at it and then comes that final shock. It's terrific." ■

[FLIGHT OF THE PHOENIX]

WRITER: Bradley Thompson & David Weddle
DIRECTOR: Michael Nankin

GUEST CAST: Jennifer Halley (Seelix), Christian Tessier (Tucker 'Duck' Clellan), Dominic Zamprogna (Jammer), Don Thompson (Specialist 3rd Class Anthony Figurski)

"Here's the deal: we are going to build a new fighter..."
— Chief Galen Tyrol

Haunted by memories of his relationship with Sharon 'Boomer' Valerii and tired of sending dilapidated Vipers to the junkyard, Chief Tyrol decides to vent his frustrations by attempting to build a new plane from salvaged parts. His off-duty mission initially generates cynicism from everyone around him, but gradually becomes a team effort for the *Galactica*'s crew.

While Tyrol's fighter takes shape, the *Galactica* is infected by a crippling computer virus that starts to wreak havoc on the Battlestar's systems. When the virus is identified by Dr Baltar as a Cylon logic bomb, Commander Adama reluctantly enlists the aid of the captive Sharon to restore *Galactica*'s systems before they are rendered defenseless against a Cylon assault. Sharon successfully transmits the virus to a nearby Cylon attack force, which immobilizes it. All of the Cylon Raiders are then destroyed by the *Galactica*'s Viper pilots.

With the crisis averted, Chief Tyrol's stealth ship is completed. The Blackbird is later publicly unveiled by President Roslin, who is touched to learn that it has been named 'Laura'.

The main storyline of 'Flight of the Phoenix' began life during season one of *Battlestar Galactica*. "Brad and I had pitched the idea of Tyrol starting to build new Vipers in the first season, because we felt it was a reality they would have to face," recalls David Weddle, who scripted the episode with Bradley Thompson. "In fact, we actually wrote some scenes for one of the first season episodes where Tyrol had built the first prototype Vipers and tried to convince reluctant pilots to fly them. But they all got cut, as so many things do, because the script was running long.

"In the second season, Ron Moore came back to the idea. But he wanted Tyrol to build just one ship and for that ship to become a focal point that rallies the sagging morale of the

Galactica's crew — bringing them together and giving them hope for the future. It then fell upon us to work out the specifics of this."

"By the time we got to this part of season two, it was emotionally the right time to do the story," adds Thompson. "We'd loaded Tyrol up with a lot of anguish and he needed to try and make sense out of this madness. People weren't making any sense, but all his life Tyrol could count on machines making sense. Building a ship was something he could control in a totally uncontrollable world. It didn't matter whether he succeeded. With every strategic item ticketed for the ships that already existed, it was an impossible challenge, one he hoped he could lose himself in. Yet the impossible nature of it would eventually drag everyone else in the crew on board."

In keeping with *Battlestar Galactica*'s ongoing quest for realism, Thompson and Weddle attempted to ensure that Tyrol's construction of the homemade Blackbird remained as plausible as possible. "We didn't believe the Chief could ever out-design the Viper company and create a super fighter from chewing gum, clapped out engines and empty birdcages," explains Thompson. "But because he couldn't get metal skins and had to use carbon composites that incidentally absorbed or scattered dradis signals, he might have a chance at creating a slow, clunky but invisible ship like the USAF F-117 Nighthawk."

Above: Tyrol's anger explodes during the opening moments of 'Flight of the Phoenix'.

Realizing that Tyrol's construction of a ship wouldn't contain many elements of jeopardy, Thompson and Weddle sought an action-orientated B-plot to form part of the episode. They found what they were looking for by picking up a plot thread from their script for the season opener, 'Scattered'.

"The Cylon logic bomb gave us a danger that could start small and get worse — and at the right moment to give us an exhilarating climax — yet not overshadow the character story of Tyrol's ship," Thompson notes. "As we played with the idea, we found it would also be a cool way to get Sharon back onto the CIC and look at all the weirdness that would produce in our crew, plus get a little payback for the Day One ass-kicking Kara's CAG took from the Cylon Raiders."

"We came up with the idea of Sharon turning the virus back on the Cylons," adds Weddle. "Ron came up with the idea of Sharon actually feeding a conduit into her arm to do this."

While finalizing the script for 'Flight of the Phoenix', Thompson and Weddle discovered that the main challenge presented by the episode was finding the right blend of its dual plotlines. "It was a very tricky balancing act to write the virus story but not to allow it to overwhelm the 'softer' story of Tyrol building the ship," says Thompson. "The emphasis shifted constantly between one story and the other from draft to draft, and this continued throughout the editorial process as Ron and David Eick finally arrived at the perfect mix."

Below: Thompson and Weddle's B-plot for 'Flight of the Phoenix' follows-up events in 'Scattered'.

A late change to the episode concerned the placing of the Blackbird's test flight. "That originally took place after the unveiling ceremony," explains Moore, "but we swapped them around during the editing, because the ceremony felt like the emotional high point of the episode."

'Flight of the Phoenix' marked Michael Nankin's first foray into the *Battlestar Galactica* universe. A veteran director as well as writer and producer, Nankin's varied credits include *Chicago Hope*, *Picket Fences*, *Invasion*, *Monk* and *American Gothic*, the series that marked his earlier collaboration with David Eick.

"Michael Nankin contributed some key ideas to the episode, including the idea of naming the Blackbird 'Laura'," Weddle reveals. "Michael also got some great performances from the actors."

Among the actors showcased by 'Flight of the Phoenix' was Aaron Douglas, whose Chief Tyrol takes center stage in its main storyline. Naturally, Douglas was thrilled by the acting opportunities presented by the episode. "I can still remember when I got the script for 'Flight of the Phoenix'," he recalls. "I was shooting episode six or seven and I got home to find a script waiting for me. I was tired but I thought I'd have a look at it, and I was just blown by it. It was basically the Tyrol show! After I read it, I sent an email to Bradley Thompson and David Weddle thanking them for it.

"I had a great time making that episode and I think it came out really well," he continues. "I enjoyed working with Michael Nankin; he's a great storyteller."

In addition to following Tyrol's construction of the Blackbird, 'Flight of the Phoenix' sees Tyrol fighting with Karl Agathon as the Chief struggles to adjust to Helo's relationship with Sharon. "We talked at length about what was going to happen when Tyrol and Helo met up," says Moore. "It seemed obvious that the first time they met, they would fight. There's a lot of rage and self-hatred in both of the characters. But I also knew I didn't want to carry that on beyond this episode. I wanted their relationship to develop in a more interesting way."

"It was fun to shoot that scene," says Douglas with a grin. "Tahmoh and I beat the hell out of each other for six hours! We did most of it ourselves."

Tyrol's struggle to find new meaning in his life clearly helped make 'Flight of the Phoenix' a uniquely touching and uplifting tale. It also provided the basis of an obvious highlight of *Battlestar Galactica*'s second season. "We were very pleased with how the show turned out," states Weddle, "and with the tremendous reaction it received." ∎

SURVEILLANCE: ADDITIONAL

'Flight of the Phoenix' was named after a 1965 war film starring James Stewart. "We are big fans of the movie," Weddle reveals. "It's a great story about pilots and leadership and teamwork — which are issues that our characters grapple with in that episode and throughout the series. And in that movie the characters take parts of a wrecked airplane and build an entirely new craft to fly themselves out of the desert, which has a thematic connection to what Tyrol and the *Battlestar* crew do in our episode."

Throughout its development and production, Ronald D. Moore also likened 'Flight of the Phoenix' to the sixth-season *M*A*S*H* installment 'War of Nerves'. The *M*A*S*H* episode opens with the show's characters facing exhaustion, but later sees them finding new purpose in life when they have to join forces to burn infected uniforms. "Ron talked about it to us repeatedly as we were writing 'Phoenix'," Weddle confirms. "We never actually saw it, but from his descriptions we understood what he wanted us to capture. Ron often refers to *M*A*S*H* — it's obviously influenced him a great deal."

[PEGASUS]

WRITER: Anne Cofell Saunders
DIRECTOR: Michael Rymer

GUEST CAST: Michelle Forbes (Admiral Helena Cain), Graham Beckel (Colonel Jack Fisk), John Pyper-Ferguson (Captain Cole 'Stinger' Taylor), Fulvio Cecere (Lt Alastair Thorne), Sebastian Spence (Pegasus Viper pilot), Vincent Gale (Chief Peter Laird), Mike Dopud (Gage), Derek Delost (Vireem), Michael Jonsson (Pegasus Guard #1)

> **"You can quote me whatever regulation you'd like. I'm not going to let you execute my men..."**
> **— Commander Adama, to Admiral Helena Cain**

The crew of the *Galactica* is overjoyed to encounter another Battlestar that survived the Cylon attack — the top-of-the-line *Pegasus*. Commanded by Admiral Helena Cain, the *Pegasus* had been tracking a Cylon Fleet on the *Galactica*'s tail prior to its discovery.

As the senior Colonial officer, Admiral Cain assumes military command of the fleet and orders the *Galactica*'s crew to assist in the planning of an attack against the mysterious vessel guarded by the pursuing Cylon Fleet. Commander Adama accepts Cain's authority and also agrees to the reassignment of key *Galactica* personnel to the *Pegasus*. At Adama's suggestion, Gaius Baltar is invited to study the *Pegasus'* resident Cylon prisoner — an abused model of Number Six, known as Gina.

When Chief Tyrol and Lieutenant Agathon learn that Sharon is about to be subjected to the same horrific treatment given to Gina, they burst into Lieutenant Thorne's interrogation. Thorne is killed in the fight that ensues.

On learning that Cain has conducted a hasty court martial for Tyrol and Agathon and sentenced them both to death for murder and treason, Adama demands his crewmen are given a full trial. Cain refuses, forcing Adama to launch the *Galactica*'s Vipers...

SURVEILLANCE: ADDITIONAL

The director's cut of 'Pegasus' featured approximately fifteen minutes of material that had to be abandoned for the episode to air in a one-hour slot. Lost scenes included Cain's explanation of why the *Pegasus'* computers were off-line during the Cylon attack (which allowed them to escape) and a discussion about Cain's quick rise to the Admiralty. "The ninety-minute version was a richer meal," says Moore. "I liked it a lot."

From the moment he agreed to remake *Battlestar Galactica*, Ronald D. Moore always planned to eventually rework the original series' two-part adventure, 'The Living Legend'. "I knew we'd have to run into the *Pegasus* at some point," he says. "But I'm glad we waited until the middle of the second season to do it, because it gave us the chance to really explore the premise. It allowed us to have another crew come over and look at how the *Galactica* has been run — and point out all the mistakes that had been made. I also wanted to wait until the *Galactica* crew was a family."

Moore initially developed the multi-episode *Pegasus* storyline with the show's writing staff, who watched 'The Living Legend' at the start of the process. "The only

Above: Admiral Cain is welcomed aboard the *Galactica* at the start of 'Pegasus'.

things we really took from the original episodes were the *Galactica* meeting the *Pegasus* and Cain," Moore notes. "One of my very first decisions was to make Cain a woman. That seemed interesting and right. The other key decision I made early on was to make Cain outrank Adama. In the original series they were both Commanders, but I felt making Cain Adama's superior officer would put us in a much better position for drama. I also thought the fact that Adama would accept Cain's authority was interesting."

While Moore considered scripting the *Pegasus* episodes himself, he ultimately felt he was too busy to do so and instead assigned the task to other writers. Anne Cofell Saunders was chosen to script the first episode of the story arc and write an outline for its concluding segment, 'Resurrection Ship'.

"'Pegasus' quite a challenge to write," says Saunders. "We wanted to introduce Admiral Cain in a way that at first brings joy and relief to *Galactica*, then, later, when her personal leadership style and philosophical approach to the Cylons becomes evident, viewers are meant to suspect that she's capable of anything."

Saunders' many additions to the storyline included details of the *Pegasus'* blind

FTL Jump and Colonel Fisk's story about the *Pegasus'* previous Executive Officer. "Laird was also a character I 'found' in the writing process," she adds. "He painted a sympathetic picture of the civilians who were drafted into service on the *Pegasus* and the terrible price they paid."

The makers of *Battlestar Galactica* were aware that the casting of Admiral Helena Cain would be crucial to the success of 'Pegasus' and 'Resurrection Ship'. A number of high-profile film stars were initially approached about the role.

"We originally chased after futile dreams like Sigourney Weaver, Jessica Lange and Angelica Huston," David Eick reveals. "But after a week of playing that game, we realized we weren't going to attract any of those actresses for a guest role, so we started looking at actresses who do television."

It was at this point that Moore, Eick and director Michael Rymer began discussing Michelle Forbes. A prolific actress who had played memorable regular and recurring roles in such TV shows as *Homicide: Life on the Street*, *24*, *Messiah*, *The Guiding Light* and *Star Trek: The Next Generation*, Forbes had also been one of the stars of the 2001 Rymer movie *Perfume*. Unfortunately, while Moore, Eick and Rymer agreed that Forbes would be ideal as Cain, they had a tough time convincing the famously selective actress to accept the role.

"When they initially offered me the role I turned it down," Forbes admits. "I didn't know the new *Battlestar Galactica* at that point and my manager had told me I wouldn't be interested, because I've played a lot of authoritarian, severe roles before and I'm always looking to do different things. So I was rather dismissive of the offer at first, out of ignorance more than anything else.

"But then they sent me about six DVDs of the show and I started watching them and I went, 'Hang on! This is good. This is *really* good. This isn't really a science fiction piece, it's more of a political/military drama.' I was struck by how much humanity and soul the series had, so I agreed to do it."

Moore, Eick and Rymer were all thrilled by Forbes' decision to sign up for the role. "I think Michelle is one of Hollywood's best-kept secrets," says Eick. "She's just amazing and magnificent as Cain. She's everything we wanted in that role."

Eick's view was quickly embraced by the show's cast, despite some initial reservations. "It's funny now," explains Rymer, "but when some of the cast heard about Michelle being

SURVEILLANCE: ADDITIONAL

'Pegasus' boasts some of season two's most moving and memorable music, courtesy of Bear McCreary. "Michael Rymer wanted to announce that this story arc would change everything," explains McCreary. "We made some unusual musical choices to help accentuate the fact that 'Pegasus' would not be 'just another episode'. Ambient electric guitar and haunting male and female vocals all found their way into this episode, along with driving ethnic percussion and woodwinds, a lonely dobro guitar and a pulse-pounding piece for string orchestra."

One of McCreary's greatest compositions for the show can be heard in the scene where Admiral Cain first visits the *Galactica*. Cain's arrival is accompanied by a haunting vocal solo by Raya Yarbrough. The song's lyrics are sung in Senegalese and are a translation of Corporal Venner's prayer from 'Scattered':

(Senegalese lyrics)	(English translation)
Dei Kobol una apita uthoukarana	Help us Lords of Kobol
Ukthea mavatha gaman kerimuta	Let us walk the path of righteousness
Obe satharane mua osavathamanabanta	And lift our faces unto your goodness
Api obata yagnya karama	We offer this prayer

hired, a couple of them went, 'So, you cast a babe...', because they knew her socially and she's a very beautiful woman. But as soon as she started working on the show, people were just saying, 'Wow! She's amazing.'"

Rymer was similarly happy with the casting of the rest of the *Pegasus*' crew. "We got a lot of fantastic actors, like Graham Beckel, John Pyper-Ferguson and Vincent Gale," he says. "They were a great bunch of people."

Commander Adama finds himself at odds with Cain and the rest of her crew during the closing part of 'Pegasus', following a brutal attack on Sharon Valerii by Lieutenant Thorne. The attempted sexual assault serves to highlight the real-life abuse of prisoners and was the subject of extensive internal debate during the episode's production. "When we shot it, we decided we were going to go beyond what had been scripted and shoot an extremely horrible, full-out assault scene," Rymer recalls. "Grace was really gung-ho about it. But when I saw it afterwards, I decided we needed to get rid of a lot of it, simply because it was so horrific. By shooting those extra moments, though, I think it gave proceedings an added sense of drama."

Above: Gaius Baltar meets the *Pegasus'* resident Number Six, Gina.

"I felt we needed to go further than what was in the script because it was an opportunity to highlight a very important real-life issue and problem," Park adds. "I was disappointed by the way it was edited down, but I know it's still a very dramatic scene."

'Pegasus' ends on a supremely dramatic note, with the *Galactica*'s Vipers poised to attack their *Pegasus* counterparts in a bid to save Tyrol and Agathon's lives. "I felt that gave us a very strong cliffhanger," Moore notes. "I also love that, once again, we see that Adama — for right or wrong — is willing to risk everything to save the men under his command. Some might say that's a profound command flaw on his part, but it also makes him a very human Commander." ■

[RESURRECTION SHIP PART I]

WRITER: Michael Rymer
STORY: Anne Cofell Saunders
DIRECTOR: Michael Rymer

GUEST CAST: Michelle Forbes (Admiral Helena Cain), Graham Beckel (Colonel Jack Fisk), John Pyper-Ferguson (Captain Cole 'Stinger' Taylor), Sebastian Spence (Pegasus Viper pilot), Vincent Gale (Chief Peter Laird), Brad Dryborough (Hoshi)

> "I'm afraid this can only end one way: you've got to kill her..."
> — President Roslin, to Commander Adama

The deadly face-off between the *Galactica* and the *Pegasus*' Viper squadrons is interrupted by the return of Lieutenant Kara 'Starbuck' Thrace, who has used the Blackbird to gain reconnaissance photos of the pursuing Cylon fleet and its mysterious main ship. With the help of Gina, the vessel is identified by Dr Baltar as a Cylon Resurrection Ship — a spacecraft which downloads the consciousnesses of dying Cylons into new bodies.

Faced with this invaluable information, Commander Adama and Admiral Cain agree to prioritize the destruction of the Resurrection Ship and forge a truce while they finalize plans for an assault on the vessel. But both officers remain distrustful of the other, especially after Adama learns that Cain ordered the *Pegasus* to abandon its civilian fleet a few months earlier.

Disturbed by this discovery, President Roslin warns Adama he must order Cain's assassination before Cain moves against him. On the eve of the strike against the Cylon Resurrection Ship, Adama reluctantly orders the *Pegasus*' new CAG, Kara Thrace, to shoot Cain immediately after the Cylon attack. As he does so, Cain orders Colonel Fisk to arrange the execution of the *Galactica*'s command crew, starting with Adama...

SURVEILLANCE: ADDITIONAL

The idea that Admiral Cain keeps her officers standing up throughout meetings was inspired by an article that Ronald D. Moore read about the US ambassador to the United Nations, John R. Bolton. It claimed that Bolton made his staff stand in meetings to ensure they didn't last too long!

'Resurrection Ship' was originally scripted and produced as a single episode of season two. But, towards the end of shooting on season two, when it became clear that the episode would require the loss of approximately twenty minutes of scenes and plot threads to fit the standard running time, the show's producers chose to expand the closing chapter of the first *Pegasus* storyline into two installments. This decision not only enabled the show to fully explore the dramatic possibilities of the storyline, but also meant that the producers could shelve their plans for a money-saving clip show.

"We were originally going to do a clip show that, in a neat way, used clips from the show to explore the nature of war and conflict as episode eighteen," David Eick recalls. "But when we hit on the idea of expanding 'Resurrection Ship' into two episodes, we instantly didn't need a clip show."

Above: Karl Agathon finds himself behind bars and facing execution.

"The original episode really lent itself to being cut into two," adds Ronald D. Moore. "By turning it into two episodes, we were able to go back and add some scenes to flesh out the storyline. We ended up with two dynamic and interesting episodes, instead of having to cut the guts out of an episode we loved."

'Resurrection Ship' marked veteran *Battlestar Galactica* director Michael Rymer's first foray into writing for the series. "I really wanted to have a crack at writing an episode," he reveals. "I'm a writer as well as a director and I felt I had contributed a lot to the writing on *Battlestar Galactica* as a director, so I asked if I could script an episode. They gave me 'Resurrection Ship' to do just after I had finished working on 'Scattered' and 'Valley of Darkness'. I was actually on my way to Italy for a holiday, so I ended up writing it when I was there."

"Michael did an amazing job writing and directing the episodes," notes Anne Cofell Saunders, who wrote the original story outline for 'Resurrection Ship' in conjunction with Moore. "Michael brings real complexity to characters and is really good at finding the emotional center of the scene."

The plotline of 'Resurrection Ship' changed significantly during the run-up to shooting. While early versions of the storyline saw Commander Adama being forced to move against Admiral Cain after she breaks her promise to protect the civilian fleet during the attack on the Cylons' Resurrection Ship, Moore realized there was a more dramatic scenario to be explored.

"I felt bringing the assassination plotline forward really made the episode a lot stronger and more interesting," he explains. "I loved Laura coming up with the idea of killing Cain and that Adama is taken aback by it. It's another of the moments where we reverse the traditional dynamics and it's completely believable. Roslin is dying and she doesn't want to leave someone as dangerous as Admiral Cain in charge of the civilian fleet.

"The scene where Laura tells Adama he must kill Cain is actually one of my favorite scenes of the season," Moore adds. "Eddie and Mary's performances are just tremendous."

Moore feels that the 'dual-assassination' plotline and the clashes between the *Galactica* and *Pegasus* crews also served to underline one of *Battlestar Galactica*'s ongoing themes. "There's always been an implication that the human characters often tend to be their own worst enemies," he notes. "A lot of the human characters' problems are of their own making and those problems are just as dangerous to them as the external threat of the Cylons."

The assassination plotline begins immediately after the previous episode's cliffhanging showdown between the *Galactica* and the *Pegasus*' Vipers is resolved. In addition to providing the basis for some top-rate and provocative drama, the assassination plotline served to reveal more about Admiral Cain. Crucially, despite her ongoing antagonism with Adama and Roslin, Cain was not portrayed as an outright villain, but instead continued to emerge as a multi-faceted character.

"I never saw Cain as a bad person," Michelle Forbes reveals. "I saw her as someone who had lost perspective. Everything that has happened since the Cylon attack has completely narrowed her vision and she's become someone who will do whatever it takes to achieve her agenda. And she's gone too far and done bad things because of that.

"It's completely believable and very relevant," she notes. "We see that in real life today, with certain people who are in charge of certain countries."

"I saw Cain as a very complicated person who was faced with a very different set of circumstances to what Adama faced," Moore agrees. "She was literally on her own and she made some hard choices that she felt had to be made. I think some of the things that she sanctioned were horrific and morally questionable to say the least, but I don't think she was a mustache-twirling villain."

Cain and Adama agree to temporarily halt their hostilities to attack the Cylon Resurrection Ship. The concept for the Resurrection Ship was originally devised during the development of the scrapped second season installment 'The Raid', a Cylon-centric episode that paved the way for 'Downloaded'. The striking look of the ship was conceived by the show's visual effects department.

SURVEILLANCE: ADDITIONAL

Although Admiral Cain was named after Lloyd Bridges' character in the original *Battlestar Galactica* two-parter 'The Living Legend', Michelle Forbes didn't base her performance on the late actor's portrayal of Commander Cain in any way. In fact, when she started working on the show, Forbes was not even aware that the 'Pegasus' and 'Resurrection Ship' three-parter had been inspired by an original series adventure. "I didn't know that was the case until about four days into shooting," she reveals. "Up to that point, I had no idea the episodes were based on a story from the original series and that I was playing Lloyd Bridges!"

"The Resurrection Ship was actually developed from one of the unused, original designs for the *Galactica*," reveals Gary Hutzel. "The original design was inspired by an architectural building in Australia that had these high arches and angles. We developed that design for the Resurrection Ship."

"It was Gary's idea to have the naked Number Sixes in the Resurrection Ship," Moore adds. "That worked really well."

The visual effects shot of the naked Number Sixes inside the Resurrection Ship was added to the episode towards the end of its production. Other late additions included Kara Thrace's flight around the Cylon vessel, which was shot months after the initial filming, when 'Resurrection Ship' became a two-parter.

"You never saw the recon mission in the original script or the original cut," Moore explains. "It worked okay like that, but it was better that we actually got to show it."

'Resurrection Ship, Part I' ends on a tense cliffhanger, with both Adama and Cain finalizing their assassination plots. Like the moment in 'Scattered' where Colonel Tigh is seen burning his medals, Cain's order to "terminate Adama's command, starting with Adama" was an homage to the classic war drama *Apocalypse Now*. Meanwhile, Adama's use of the word "downfall" as the code for Cain's execution is a nod to the award-winning 2004 German film about Hitler's last days. ∎

Above: Kara Thrace forms a close bond with Admiral Cain as the 'Pegasus' story arc develops.

[RESURRECTION SHIP PART II]

WRITERS: Michael Rymer & Ronald D. Moore
DIRECTOR: Michael Rymer

GUEST CAST: Michelle Forbes (Admiral Helena Cain), Graham Beckel (Colonel Jack Fisk), Vincent Gale (Chief Peter Laird), Brad Dryborough (Hoshi), Derek Delost (Vireem), Mike Dopud (Gage), James Chutter (Marine Honor Guard)

"Tens of thousands of Cylons are about to die..." — Number Six

On the eve of the assault on the Cylon Resurrection Ship, Lee Adama is wracked with doubt over his father's plans to assassinate Admiral Cain. He confronts the Commander about his decision and is shocked to learn that Cain's execution was actually President Roslin's idea.

When the mission begins, Lee flies the Blackbird into the heart of the Resurrection Ship and successfully disables its FTL drive, which allows the *Galactica* and *Pegasus*' Vipers to attack and destroy the vessel. But the Blackbird is damaged during the mission and Lee is left floating in space. With his oxygen supply rapidly depleting, Lee loses the will to live and gives up his battle for life. However, Lee is saved at the last minute by a Raptor crew, who successfully revive him.

Following the destruction of the Resurrection Ship, Adama decides he cannot order Cain's assassination. Cain, meanwhile, surprises her Executive Officer by abandoning her plans to execute *Galactica*'s command crew.

As the crews celebrate their victory over the Cylons, Baltar releases Gina from the *Pegasus*' brig. During her escape, Gina confronts and kills Admiral Cain. In the wake of Cain's demise, President Roslin appoints Adama as the new military leader of the fleet and promotes him to the rank of Admiral...

Opposite: The Adama-Roslin kiss at the end of 'Resurrection Ship, Part II' was improvised by Edward James Olmos.

SURVEILLANCE: ADDITIONAL

Gina was named by Moore as a nod to die-hard fans of the original *Battlestar Galactica* who refer to the new series as '*Galactica* in name only'!

Ronald D. Moore always had a clear idea of how the *Pegasus* storyline would conclude. "I knew from the start that the audience would assume the *Pegasus* would be destroyed or lost, as in the original series," he notes. "So I decided right away that we'd go in another direction and keep the *Pegasus* around.

"Cain, however, was doomed from the start," he continues with a grin. "We never seriously discussed keeping the character until after we'd shot the episodes and realized what a great job Michelle Forbes had done. We all kind of went, 'You know what? It's a shame we killed her off!'"

As co-scripted by Moore and director Michael Rymer, 'Resurrection Ship, Part II' opens with a glimpse of the *Galactica* and *Pegasus*' joint assault on the Cylon Resurrection Ship, which is shown in its entirety later in the episode. The battle is mostly viewed from the perspective of Captain Lee Adama, as he fights for his life after ejecting into space

from the Blackbird. "We wanted to find a different way of doing a battle sequence," says Moore of the thinking behind the scene. "The idea was inspired by a true story from World War II about a pilot called Ensign George Gay, who was shot down during the battle of Midway and witnessed the entire battle from the water, in his little life jacket."

"I know some people felt disappointed they didn't get to just see the battle," Rymer acknowledges. "But, personally, I felt we didn't need to see another big battle from scratch and that it was secondary to the main story between the Commander and the Admiral."

Lee Adama's actions while watching the battle were the subject of intense controversy among *Battlestar Galactica*'s makers. Originally, the producers planned to show Lee purposely trying to kill himself after he found himself surrounded by dead bodies floating in space and was struck by a feeling of despair and futility. But this crucial sequence — which sets the scene for Lee's arc for the rest of the season — went through several revisions before it reached the air.

"We shot it and re-shot it, cut it and re-cut it," Jamie Bamber reveals. "Lee was originally going to face an existential crisis and commit suicide, but there were concerns about that, so we had to cut it down. It became much more ambiguous about whether he's committing suicide or simply realizing he can't do anything to save himself because of the oxygen loss and just accepting that's he going to die anyway.

"I understand why they changed it," he adds. "You have to tread carefully because you don't want to rip out the heart of a character — it might not serve the whole show."

Following the attack on the Resurrection Ship, the rest of the episode focuses on resolving the assassination plot. The revelation that neither Adama nor Cain can order the murder of the other allowed Moore to come back to one of the series' central themes — the idea that humanity must strive to be worthy of survival — and also showed a different side of Cain.

"I really like how Cain redeems herself a little bit in the end," says 'Pegasus' writer Anne Cofell Saunders. "We see that she is capable of mercy and has a human streak."

Sadly for viewers (if not the show's characters), Cain's reprieve was short-lived. Shortly after the destruction of the Resurrection Ship, the character is killed by Gina. Moore and Rymer initially discussed having Gina walk into the *Pegasus*' CIC and shoot the entire command crew, before settling on a more simple and direct confrontation between her and Cain.

"I thought my death scene was pretty good," says Forbes with a chuckle. "It was a wonderfully interesting and complex moment to play, because we see this woman who has become fanatic about wiping out the Cylons dying at the hands of a Cylon."

SURVEILLANCE: ADDITIONAL

During the development of the *Pegasus* story arc, Moore initially toyed with Admiral Cain simply refusing to accept President Roslin's authority and considered depicting a clash between the *Pegasus* and the civilian fleet over resources. Moore and the show's writing staff also discussed the possibility of a full battle erupting between the *Galactica* and *Pegasus*' Vipers at the end of 'Pegasus', but decided that once shots had been fired there was no chance of a truce being forged between the two crews.

One thing Moore never considered, however, was giving Admiral Cain a daughter, like in the original *Battlestar Galactica*. "I felt Sheba was too cute a character for our show," he explains. "I thought it would be too much of a stretch for the reality of the show. It worked for the original series, but not for us."

Cain's funeral was among the new scenes that were shot when 'Resurrection Ship' became a two-parter. Other additions included the scene between Cain and Kara Thrace that underlines the growing bond between the two characters and the sequence in which the imprisoned Tyrol and Agathon are beaten by *Pegasus* crewmen. The latter scene was loosely inspired by the beatings and threatened beatings featured in the movies *Full Metal Jacket* and *The Grifters*, and — following the characters' discussion in 'Resurrection Ship, Part I' — served to emphasize the idea that Tyrol and Agathon would no longer be at odds with each other over Sharon Valerii.

Above: Michelle Forbes felt that 'Resurrection Ship, Part II' gave her character a very fitting death scene.

"A triangle between Tyrol, Helo and Sharon seemed too easy," Moore explains. "We didn't want to go there. Tyrol and Helo had separate experiences with literally two separate Sharons. So even though Tyrol definitely has conflicted thoughts and feelings about it, his overall arc for the rest of the season was to try to get away from Sharon and put it 'all behind him."

The *Pegasus* story arc ends with Roslin promoting Adama to the rank of Admiral. "I thought that was an unexpected end to the episode," Moore notes. "I really like the affection you see between Roslin and Adama in the scene. Eddie improvised the kiss — he just did it because of the emotion he was feeling in that scene — and you can kind of see the surprise in Mary's face."

"It felt very natural for the characters to share a physical moment," McDonnell adds. "Laura is on the verge of death and it's a very emotional time for both them."

'Resurrection Ship, Part II' would ultimately become widely regarded as a fitting finale to the *Pegasus* story arc. "I was impressed by all three of the episodes I did," says Forbes. "I think *Battlestar Galactica* is one of the smartest shows on television right now and I was so moved by the episodes. I admired their bravery in addressing issues raised by times of war and I thought Michael Rymer did an amazing job of hitting all the points. I just feel honored that I got to be a part of it."

"I think the 'Resurrection Ship' episodes are interesting and strong shows," Rymer notes. "But I think 'Pegasus' is an exceptional episode. That was one of my personal favorites — for me, it's up there alongside '33' and the 'Kobol's Last Gleaming' episodes." ∎

[EPIPHANIES]

WRITER: Joel Anderson Thompson
DIRECTOR: Rod Hardy

GUEST CAST: Colm Feore (President Richard Adar), Paul Perri (Royan Jahee), David Richmond-Peck (Naylin Stans), Holly Dignard (Asha Janik), Jennifer Kitchen (Marine)

"Allowing this thing to be born could have frightening consequences. For the security of this fleet, I believe the Cylon pregnancy must be terminated..." — President Roslin

President Laura Roslin lies dying in the *Galactica*'s sickbay. When Dr Cottle informs her that he has detected unusual genetic properties in the blood of Sharon Valerii's unborn Cylon-human baby, Roslin feels she has no choice but to order its termination. But before the procedure can take place, Dr Baltar discovers he can use the baby's blood to cure Roslin's cancer.

Meanwhile, Chief Tyrol discovers that the Vipers' ammunition has been sabotaged. The action is traced to an underground movement that seeks peace with the Cylons. Admiral Adama arrests the group's leader, Royan Jahee, but that does not stop his followers from bombing the Tylium refinery. Baltar is later contacted by a member of the peace movement, Gina, and secretly arranges for her to receive a nuclear weapon as a token of his goodwill.

As Roslin recovers, she remembers the vivid visions she experienced on her deathbed. These included seeing Baltar with Number Six on Caprica shortly before the Cylon attack...

Opposite: Sharon's unborn baby is marked for death by President Roslin.

SURVEILLANCE: ADDITIONAL

At one point in the development of 'Epiphanies', it was suggested that the meeting Number Six refers to in the miniseries was actually with Laura Roslin, rather than another humanoid Cylon. "We talked about working that in as a reveal in the 'Epiphanies' flashbacks," explains Moore, "but we couldn't come up with any rational justification for why Laura wouldn't have reacted to the Shelley Godfrey Cylon in 'Six Degrees of Separation'."

'Epiphanies' was prompted by Ronald D. Moore's desire to resolve — at least for the time being — Laura Roslin's battle with cancer. "I originally wanted to keep that going until the end of the series," Moore reveals. "But as we got deeper into the show and played that illness as believably as we could, it felt like we either had to kill Laura or take it off the table altogether. Laura is such a vibrant part of the show that we just went, 'Okay, let's just bite the bullet and take it off the table and move on.' So that's what we did."

Determined that Roslin's cancer wouldn't be cured by Colonial science or some newly-discovered alien technology, Moore embraced the suggestion that the key to Roslin's survival would be found in Sharon Valerii's unborn baby. He initially toyed with the idea that the baby's stem cells would provide the basis of the cure, as he felt it would allow the show to address the real-world controversy surrounding stem sell research. But Moore ultimately dropped this idea, in an attempt to keep the episode's focus on human drama rather than science.

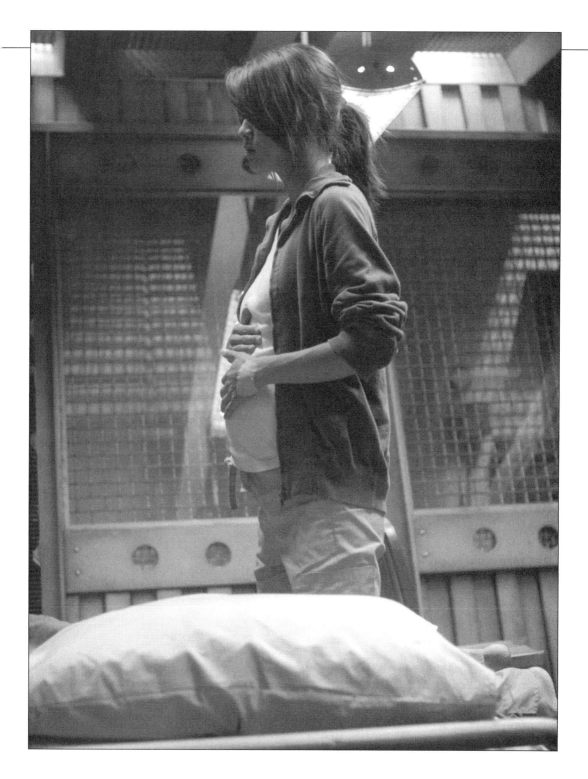

"The storyline came together quite easily," he recalls. "There was a nice symmetry to the fact that the unborn Cylon child could save Laura, and that Baltar would be the one to figure that out. The episode also provided us with an opportunity to explore Laura's back-story using flashbacks. We wanted to explore who she was and what she was like before the attack on Caprica."

The task of scripting Roslin's return to health fell on *Battlestar Galactica*'s executive story editor, Joel Anderson Thompson. "My main goal for the episode was to have President Roslin set on executing the unborn Cylon baby for the theoretical good of the human race, only to experience a moment of reversal and recognition on the most personal level possible," he notes. "How can killing a Cylon be the only answer if one needs a Cylon to stay alive? This paradox of reasoning forces Laura to recalibrate how she defines humanity not just as a concept but for herself biologically."

'Epiphanies' was the fourth episode of *Battlestar Galactica* to be directed by Rod Hardy. Shooting the episode proved to be an extremely memorable experience for Mary McDonnell, who savored the dramatic challenges presented by its storyline.

"The thing I remember most clearly about that episode was the very admirable atmosphere that Rod Hardy created on-set," she explains. "He was so completely unafraid of photographing a woman dying of cancer and he allowed us to play it for real. There was a real feeling in the room that the President was dying. And when we shot the scenes with Laura ordering the termination of Sharon's baby, there was a real sense of commitment on the set."

Prior to shooting 'Epiphanies', McDonnell questioned whether Laura really would order the termination of Sharon's unborn child, but she was assured by Moore it was a logical development for the character. "It was in line with all the other decisions that Laura had made up to that point," he explains. "She knew time was running out and she felt very rightly she could not leave the decision in Baltar's hands."

As Roslin fights for life, she recalls her tempestuous relationship with President Adar. The idea that Adar and Roslin had been lovers was prompted by Roslin's line in the miniseries where she noted she had always found it hard to say no to the former President. Adar was played by Colm Feore, a veteran stage and screen actor whose many credits include the movies *The Chronicles of Riddick* and *Paycheck*.

"Colm was just wonderful to work with," says McDonnell. "He came in with a really theatrical energy. He's such a talented actor and a charming man, it was a pleasure to have him around on that episode. All the women on the set, in particular, really loved him."

The B-plot to 'Epiphanies' was devised by Anderson, who pitched the idea of a storyline involving Cylon sympathizers among the Colonial fleet at his very first creative meeting with the show's makers at the start of season two. "'Epiphanies' was an opportunity to harvest another creative germ from American history," he reveals. "The idea of Cylon sympathizers was a concept born from the renegade abolitionist John Brown's violent anti-slavery effort of the 1800s.

"The Cylon sympathizer storyline also had a secondary purpose that was important to me," he continues. "It indirectly posed the question: are the Cylons really the bad guys here or are the humans facing annihilation as a price for their sins? That's why we were careful not to have the sympathizers depicted with any arch villainous characteristics. When Lee and Kara apprehend one sympathizer, she's hard at work shoulder to shoulder with other people. The 'living and working among us' angle, in some ways, makes them more frightening and, hopefully, it leaves one more inclined to think about who these people are and why they are willing to kill to make their point. The black-and-white questions can be easier to negotiate. I think it's the shades-of-gray questions that get our creative juices going."

Moore responded to Anderson's idea about Cylon sympathizers, as he felt it was unusual for a space opera to employ members of a peace movement as antagonists. The show runner encouraged Anderson to build on the real-world parallels by having the Cylon sympathizers employ similar tactics to World War II prisoners of war who were forced to work for the Nazis and attempted to sabotage ammunition.

The Cylon sympathizer storyline also served to reunite Baltar with Gina and continue their relationship. Early in the script's development, a love scene was planned between the two characters, but it was later dropped at Tricia Helfer's request. "Tricia felt that wasn't appropriate for Gina after what had happened to her on the *Pegasus*," Moore recalls. "We agreed and we also felt it put Baltar in an interesting place, because he wouldn't be able to consummate that relationship."

'Epiphanies' closes with Baltar giving Gina the nuclear bomb that had been part of his Cylon detector, in a development that sets the scene for events in the season's closing episode. "It was fun to finally come back to the nuclear weapon," says Moore. "We'd been talking about doing something with it ever since the middle of season one and we always wanted to address that plot thread." ∎

Above: Roslin's flashback to Baltar and Number Six on Caprica sets up events in the season's closing episode.

[BLACK MARKET]

WRITER: Mark Verheiden
DIRECTOR: James Head

GUEST CAST: Bill Duke (Phelan), Graham Beckel (Colonel Jack Fisk), Claudette Mink (Shevon), Hayley Guiel (Paya), Brad Mann (Pegasus Marine), James Ashcroft (Security Officer), Amy Lalonde (Gianne), Gustavo Febres (Herbalist)

> **"There are lines you can't cross, and you've crossed them..."**
> **— Captain Adama, to Phelan**

hen Colonel Jack Fisk is found brutally murdered, Admiral Adama asks his son to investigate the death of the *Pegasus*' commanding officer. Lee discovers a cache of cigarettes, liquor and jewelry in Fisk's quarters, which links him to the fleet's black market — an illegal trade system that serves the rich and deprives the needy of essential goods.

The investigation into Fisk's death becomes personal for Lee when Shevon, a prostitute he had been spending time with, is kidnapped with her young daughter, Paya. Lee learns that the black market's leader, Phelan, is responsible for their disappearance and is told that they will not be harmed if he abandons his search for Fisk's murderer.

Reminded of how he abandoned his pregnant girlfriend shortly before the Cylon attack on Caprica, Lee feels he cannot leave Shevon in Phelan's hands. With the help of Tom Zarek, he locates Phelan on the renegade freighter, the *Prometheus*, and kills him. He then tells Phelan's associates that the black market will continue, but will no longer interfere with essential medicines or encompass murder or child slavery.

With Shevon and her daughter safe, Lee hopes to resume their relationship. Instead, however, Shevon tells him that she cannot be a replacement for the woman he abandoned on Caprica and says they should no longer see each other...

SURVEILLANCE: ADDITIONAL

The original *Battlestar Galactica* featured a prostitute as one of its main characters. Labeled a 'Socialator', the character was called Cassiopeia. "She was played by Laurette Sprang, who every adolescent boy watching the show had a crush on," notes Ronald D. Moore. "I know because I was one of them!"

'Black Market' provided an opportunity to shine the spotlight on one of *Battlestar Galactica*'s main characters, as well as reveal more about life in the Colonial fleet. "We wanted to explore the Lee Adama character in that episode," explains writer Mark Verheiden. "He had just been through some serious emotional changes, including a near-death experience in outer space, and it seemed like a good time to see why he was so conflicted about flying and the military. We wanted to show flashes of Lee's personal history, including his failed engagement on Caprica just before the Cylon attack. It always seemed to me that Lee's back-story was one of the least fleshed out among the main characters, and this was a chance to finally understand this guy's motivations.

"I was also interested in exploring the emergence of a flourishing black market and seeing how that impacted people in an already dire situation," he continues. "I find the

details of life in the fleet endlessly fascinating, and one of the wonderful aspects of *Battlestar* is that we can go to these dark, morally messed-up places without necessarily cleaning everything up by the show's end."

"The storyline came out of some interesting discussions about what would be happening in the fleet, economically," adds Moore. "When we were talking about how people were getting things, we came up with the idea of a black market that would be withholding essential items and interfering with the rationing system. But the episode is primarily a Lee story: it's Lee going up the river, like in Joseph Conrad's *Heart of Darkness*, and ultimately finding Kurtz in Phelan.

"I thought the idea that Lee was seeing a prostitute was very interesting," he adds. "You don't often see the classic clean-cut good guy having a relationship with a hooker."

The premise of 'Black Market' was embraced by Jamie Bamber, who welcomed the opportunity to explore his character's past and present. But Bamber readily admits that he was initially concerned about certain aspects of the episode's storyline. "When I read the script and saw that Lee had been seeing a prostitute for a few months, I did think to myself that was a bit strong," he recalls with a laugh. "I was also shocked that he shoots a person in cold blood. So I did find myself wondering about the effect these things would have on the character and the show, but it took me all of an hour to realize that, in many ways, the episode was the best thing that had ever happened to my character. It was great to see Lee pushed into a really extreme position; Lee is arguably the conscience of the show, so it was exciting to see him pushed into such a dark position that he almost loses his conscience.

"I loved working on the episode," Bamber adds. "I don't think I've ever done an hour of television before where I was in almost every scene. It was also a brave departure for the show. There had never been a one-plot episode before."

'Black Market' marked the *Battlestar Galactica* début of director James Head, who had previously directed episodes of such shows as *Stargate: Atlantis*, *The Commish*, *The Dead Zone* and *Gene Roddenberry's Earth: Final Conflict*. In a coup for the series, the episode's villain was played by Bill Duke. A distinguished character actor and director, Duke's many credits include *Get Rich Or Die Tryin'*, *Payback*, *Bird on a Wire*, *Commando*, *Predator* and *X-Men: The Last Stand* (which was partly shot on the same Vancouver studio lot as *Battlestar Galactica*).

"Bill Duke is a great actor and a great director," Moore notes. "Casting him in that role was wonderful because he brought a real presence to the show — you know his character is capable of bad things."

One aspect of 'Black Market' that Moore particularly liked was the shocking nature of Phelan's demise. This idea actually came from US Sci Fi Channel executive Mark Stern, who suggested Lee should kill Phelan in cold blood on reading an early version of the episode's storyline. "That's probably the best moment in the episode," says Moore. "Having the hero simply shoot the villain is a really unexpected thing to do and it's more complicated than the clean-cut comfort of most TV. It was a great suggestion from Mark."

Moore was similarly happy with the episode's confrontation between Lee Adama and Colonel Tigh, and the scene where Adama tells his father and President Roslin about the deal he has brokered with the black market criminals, in an exchange that echoes the conclusion of season one's 'Bastille Day'. He also liked the way the episode subtly progresses Baltar's move towards pursuing the Presidency, with a scene in which he refuses to take Roslin's advice and resign as Vice President.

Yet despite its obvious strengths, 'Black Market' fell short of Moore's initial expectations. On viewing the footage, he felt extremely disappointed with the episode and made several changes to it in editing, including moving a

SURVEILLANCE: ADDITIONAL

Ronald D. Moore has defended his decision to have Admiral Adama remain on the *Galactica*, rather than lead the fleet from the *Pegasus*. "There's ample precedent for admirals to hoist their flags aboard vessels that are not necessarily the biggest and most powerful in the fleet," says Moore. "Raymond Spruance, Commander of the US Fifth Fleet in World War II, often kept his flag aboard the USS *Indianapolis*, a heavy cruiser, rather than one of the fleet's carriers or battleships, simply because he used to command cruisers and felt more comfortable there... So Adama has kept his flag aboard *Galactica* because it's his ship and he doesn't want to move."

glimpse of Lee's final confrontation with Phelan to the teaser. But by the time of the episode's completion, neither Moore nor David Eick were satisfied with the finished product.

"'Black Market' is not an episode I particularly like," Moore admits. "I take responsibility for it as the head writer and an executive producer on the show. I don't think it fits well into the show. It's just too conventional a tale and too conventional in its execution. You know where the episode is going to go from the start. I liked the script — Mark Verheiden is a very good writer — and there were some good ideas in there, but it all just didn't really gel."

"We weren't wrong to do an episode about a black market or the pathos of Lee's history," Eick says. "Conceptually it was all very interesting and good. But the episode just didn't come together the way it might have."

Moore and Eick's disappointment was shared by Jamie Bamber. "When I watched the finished episode, I didn't like it," he reveals. "I really enjoyed the experience of shooting it and felt challenged by trying to hold a story together, but in the end I felt that something was missing. The two story strands weren't fleshed out enough — and, as a result, it was hard to say what the episode was about."

Above: Lee reluctantly makes a deal with Phelan's associates during the climax of 'Black Market'.

Ultimately, 'Black Market' was an episode that divided audiences: while some viewers shared Moore and Eick's verdict, others — including the show's principal director, Michael Rymer — really enjoyed it. "It was a somewhat 'controversial' episode," Verheiden agrees. "Some folks reacted well to the whole film noir-ish concept, while others — including, unfortunately, Ron — did not.

"I find myself somewhere in the middle," he reveals. "It's not my favorite episode but there are some nice moments, with good work from Jamie Bamber and James Callis. It was an odd experience because the response to the script was very positive, but somehow what we liked there just didn't translate totally on screen." ■

[SCAR]

WRITERS: Bradley Thompson & David Weddle
DIRECTOR: Michael Nankin

GUEST CAST: Christian Tessier (Tucker 'Duck' Clellan), Sean Dory (Ensign Joseph 'Jo-Jo' Clark), Christopher Jacot (Ensign Brent 'BB' Baxton)

"I am hung up on a dead guy, okay, and it is pissing me off. And I don't know what I'm doing..." — Lieutenant Thrace

The crew of the Colonial mining ship *Majahual* has been working round the clock for a month, extracting essential metals from an asteroid. Their mission is observed by the *Galactica*'s Viper pilots, who have to protect the miners from persistent Cylon raids. The pilots' deadliest foe is a Cylon Raider nicknamed 'Scar', a master of hit-and-run attacks who has been decimating the *Galactica*'s Viper squadrons.

Following a tense confrontation between Kara 'Starbuck' Thrace and Louanne 'Kat' Katraine, the two Viper pilots embark on a fierce competition to kill Scar. With Kara haunted by memories of Anders, she increasingly hits the bottle and almost sleeps with Lee Adama.

Kara and Kat finally confront Scar together and Kara enables Kat to destroy the Cylon. Kat is crowned the *Galactica*'s new top gun, while Starbuck realizes she cannot give up hope on Anders...

Initially nicknamed "the *Red Baron* episode" by *Battlestar Galactica*'s writing staff, 'Scar' provided writers Bradley Thompson and David Weddle with another excellent vehicle for their extensive knowledge of real-life military procedures and combat tactics, as well as the springboard for some rich character-based drama. "Ron Moore wanted us to do an episode that really took viewers into the world of the fighter pilots and showed what their lives were really like," says Thompson of the genesis of 'Scar'. "He wanted us to show the stress of flying a Viper and how it's not all fun and games. That was something that had always interested David and I; our first episode, 'Act of Contrition', also touched on the lives of the Viper pilots. David Eick also wanted to do an episode that saw Kara going up against Kat in a competition, so we used their rivalry to defeat a really deadly Cylon Raider as the basis of the drama."

"The episode really takes Kara down a peg," Moore adds. "We never wanted Starbuck to be perfect and there was something cool about taking the one thing she really prided herself on away from her for a moment, or making her decide she didn't want to be top gun any more. It roughs up the character more and makes her more interesting and complicated."

During the scripting of 'Scar', Thompson and Weddle were required to find a way of

Opposite: 'Scar' forces Kara Thrace to confront her demons - and also reveals the extent of her friendship with Karl Agathon.

SURVEILLANCE: ADDITIONAL

'Scar' establishes that the consciousnesses of destroyed Cylon Raiders can be downloaded into new Raiders.

depicting the competition between Kara and Kat without featuring a series of expensive space-battle sequences. "Ron said we could only have one big combat sequence," Weddle explains, "so we had to find other venues of competition. That led to us coming up with things like the characters' clashes in the briefings and the Firing Range competition."

The Firing Range contest centers on the pilots' struggle with G-forces and dizziness in a space-flight simulator chair. Inspired by a real-life vertigo simulator that Thompson encountered while visiting Edwards Air Force Base, this prop was realized using a chair from one of the show's Vipers. "The guys did a phenomenal job building this gyroscopic chair that spins on both axes," says Douglas McLean. "When they got the actors and stunt people in it, it was very effective."

As helmed by 'Flight of the Phoenix' director Michael Nankin, 'Scar' was destined to be a memorable showcase for Katee Sackhoff — although Sackhoff herself admits to having mixed feelings about the episode. "I thought 'Scar' was a great episode in many respects," she explains. "I thought it was brilliantly written and Michael Nankin is a great director, and I really liked a lot of the episode. But I hated it that Kat became top gun!

"Maybe that's just the part of me that's Starbuck speaking," she continues, "but I didn't buy it. I told the producers it didn't make sense to me; I thought it would be better if it had been a pilot we hadn't seen before, like someone on the *Pegasus*, rather than Kat, who hadn't actually been a pilot that long. But they were determined to do it — they wanted it to be someone the audience already knew."

Despite her concerns about Kat's elevation to the position of *Galactica*'s top gun, Sackhoff enjoyed portraying Starbuck's bitter rivalry with the character. Sackhoff's appreciation for those scenes was shared by Luciana Carro, who was excited to play such a big role in the episode. "I was jumping up and down for joy when I first read the script for 'Scar'," she reveals, "especially when I read the bit where Kat becomes top gun and the pilots are cheering, 'Kat! Kat! Kat!' I was really surprised and honored that my character was going to become top gun.

"It was a fun episode to do," she continues. "Michael Nankin is a wonderful director and working with Katee was terrific. She's a fantastic actress and a very strong presence, so going up against her in those scenes was terrific because it keeps you on your toes. You have to match her, or else she'll take you down!"

Another major character development in 'Scar' concerns Kara's attempted sexual encounter with Lee Adama, which addresses the attraction between the two characters but also helps Kara realize her love for Anders. "People had talked about Starbuck and Apollo getting it on since the miniseries," says Moore. "I always wanted them to get it on at some point, but in a

SURVEILLANCE: ADDITIONAL

David Weddle first suggested naming season two's fifteenth episode 'Scar'. "It felt right because it addressed on many levels what Kara was going through in the episode," says Bradley Thompson, "and because the easiest way to recognize one Raider out of many was to give it battle scars."

Although the episode shares its name with the Native American antagonist in *The Searchers*, it was not a deliberate homage to the classic John Ford Western. "'Scar' wasn't specifically a reference to *The Searchers*," says Thompson, "but the film is never far from our minds. Certainly it has a thematic similarity in that Kara is chasing an enemy that has more humanity than she's comfortable admitting."

very screwed-up way."

"Before we shot that scene, Jamie Bamber and I said to each other, 'Let's make this scene so tragic that they can't go back to how things were afterwards'," Sackhoff says of Starbuck's attempted liaison with Apollo. "We shot that scene a bit like a fight — it's rough and aggressive. I was covered in bruises after we shot it!"

Following Kat's naming as the

Above: A drunken Kara turns to Lee Adama for solace - with traumatic results.

Galactica's new top gun, Kara leads a toast to the Battlestar's dead pilots — and finds herself overcome with emotion and unable to finish. Although Thompson, Weddle and Moore's podcast for the episode claimed that this moment was improvised on set, the writers have since discovered that actually wasn't the case. "We looked back at the script after doing the podcast and discovered that the moment where Kara can't continue and Lee picks up the ball was scripted," explains Thompson. "But that doesn't take anything away from the brilliant work by Michael Nankin and the cast on that scene."

The closing moments of 'Scar' see Kara discussing her love for Anders with Karl Agathon, in a scene that cements his position as one of her most trusted friends. "That was a beautiful scene," says Tahmoh Penikett. "It shows that Helo is one of the few people who can say certain things to Starbuck, because he knows her so well. It really shows the bond between those two characters."

Agathon's discussion with Kara is accompanied by 'Cavatina', a guitar solo most famously featured in the 1978 movie *The Deer Hunter*. The episode's use of the piece was first suggested by David Eick. "I was watching an early cut of the episode and I just thought that great acoustic guitar solo would be perfect for that scene," Eick recalls. "So I asked them to try it and it worked better than I expected. I then took the idea to the studio and they got behind it and got us the money to make it happen."

After the completion of shooting on 'Scar', the episode required extensive editing to ensure its complex flashback-driven structure worked in a coherent and dramatic fashion. Many of Michael Nankin's unscripted additions made it into the final cut, such as the scene where a pilot is sick as he leaves his Viper, while the final dogfight scene between Kara, Kat and Scar was simplified to ensure viewers could follow it.

"It was a difficult show to make work," says Moore. "But we were all in love with the episode and worked overtime to make it work. It came out really well — it's one of the best episodes of the season."

"Bradley and I are very proud of 'Scar'," Weddle concludes. "Michael Nankin did a great job of bringing the episode to life and Katee Sackhoff is amazing." ∎

[SACRIFICE]

WRITER: Anne Cofell Saunders
DIRECTOR: Reynaldo Villalobos

GUEST CAST: Dana Delany (Sesha Abinell), Mark Houghton (Kern Vinson), David Neale (Nelson Page), Eric Breker (George Chu), Michael Ryan (Ray Abinell), Adrian Hughes (Lt Terry 'Gunnery' Burrell), James Upton (Environmental Specialist), Erica Carroll (Civilian)

"I'm not going to sacrifice a military asset on your altar of revenge" — Admiral Adama, to Sesha Abinell

Haunted by her husband's death in a recent Cylon raid, Sesha Abinell takes the occupants of a *Cloud Nine* bar hostage. Abinell and her group demand that the Cylon Sharon Valerii is surrendered to them for execution and they warn Admiral Adama that they will kill their hostages — who include Lee Adama, Anastasia Dualla, Billy Keikeya and Ellen Tigh — if he does not comply.

When Lee secretly manages to fake a malfunction on the ship's air supply system, Kara Thrace poses as an engineer to lead a strike against Abinell. But Kara and her marines only manage to kill one of Abinell's group and Lee is accidentally shot by Kara during the shoot-out.

With time running out for his son, Adama agrees to give Abinell what she wants — but really hands over the dead body of Sharon 'Boomer' Valerii. As Abinell realizes Boomer is not the Sharon that has been aiding Admiral Adama, Adama's marines make their move against her — as does Billy. Abinell and her conspirators are shot and killed, but not before Billy is fatally wounded.

While Admiral Adama and President Roslin grieve for Billy, Dualla watches over Lee as he recovers from his near-fatal shooting...

'Sacrifice' was conceived as the episode that marked Paul Campbell's final appearance as Billy Keikeya. "For contractual reasons, Paul was still available to work on other shows and it had become problematic, because we didn't know if we had him or not," explains Ronald D. Moore. "We decided to write the character out of the show and the logical thing was to kill Billy, because it didn't make sense for him to just decide to leave or go live on some other ship.

"It wasn't an easy thing to do," he continues. "Billy was one of my favorite characters and Paul was a very popular member of our cast. But Paul was being offered lead roles in other series and movie projects while in our show he was a supporting player, so we felt it was better for both him and us if we went ahead and wrote him out."

"I had been offered a five-year contract on *Battlestar Galactica*, but I wasn't sure I wanted to commit to it," Campbell reveals. "If I was going to sign up to something for that

Above: Kara Thrace's unsuccessful rescue mission proved to be one of the more interesting elements of 'Sacrifice'.

long, I'd like to be playing a really meaty, center-of-the-action role, and Billy was never going to be that. I think David Eick and Ron Moore realized that, so they called me to the office one day and told me Billy was no more. They were concerned about my availability, and I think it was a totally just decision. I wasn't expecting it to be so soon — I thought I'd last the rest of the season — but that's the business."

Marking the *Battlestar Galactica* directorial début of veteran TV helmer and cinematographer Reynaldo Villalobos (*Wiseguy, Tour of Duty*), 'Sacrifice' was an episode that changed considerably during its journey from page to screen. Originally entitled 'The Enemy Within', the Anne Cofell Saunders-scripted siege drama was initially set on a military shuttle that was taken over by Cylon-hating terrorists. The group's hostages included Billy, Ellen Tigh, Jammer and Laird, but not Lee Adama or Dualla. As the storyline continued, a conflict developed between Admiral Adama and Colonel Tigh that culminated in Tigh raising a gun to his superior officer.

"We originally wanted Tigh to go toe-to-toe with Adama over his refusal to hand over Sharon and the way it was putting Ellen's life in danger," explains Moore, "but we just couldn't get to a point where it was believable. We'd established Tigh and Adama were such close friends and trusted comrades that it just didn't work. It was similar to what we experienced with season one's 'Tigh Me Up, Tigh Me Down'."

"'Sacrifice' changed a lot during its development," Saunders confirms. "But the most important aspect of the script for me was to give Paul Campbell a solid, heroic death."

Saunders' script for 'Sacrifice' also represented the culmination of the love triangle between Billy, Dualla and Lee that had been established in the earlier season two episodes 'Resistance' and 'Flight of the Phoenix'. "We'd been talking about playing a classic romantic triangle among some of the characters, even before Billy was going," Moore recalls, "and it seemed like a good direction for those particular characters."

One of the last additions to the episode's script was Kara Thrace's accidental shooting of Lee during her botched strike against the terrorists. "It was always part of the script that Lee was shot in that sequence, but it wasn't until late in the process that someone suggested Kara should be the one that shot him," explains Moore. "I loved that idea because it gave Kara more angst to deal with, and it became one of my favorite aspects of the episode."

Throughout the development of 'Sacrifice', the siege was always orchestrated by Sesha Abinell. The character's creation was prompted by Moore's belief that the fleet's civilian population would speculate about what had really happened to Sharon Valerii and that some people would conclude that there was a Cylon collaborator somewhere in the military. David Eick suggested former *China Beach* star Dana Delany would be excellent as Abinell and was thrilled when Delany accepted an offer from the production.

"I've been friends with Dana Delaney for years," he reveals, "and we'd been looking for a role for her for some time. I think we'd talked to her about other roles in the past, like Ellen Tigh, and it was great that she agreed to do this episode. Dana is just one of those actresses who elevates whatever piece of television she's doing. She's a class piece of talent and she conjures this idea of quality, just like Meryl Streep does in a movie."

Two other aspects of 'Sacrifice' that remained constant during the episode's development were its exploration of Adama's conflicted feelings towards Sharon Valerii and its focus on the mystery surrounding Sharon's true motivations. "The episode asks what Sharon's presence means to our characters and what she's all about," Moore notes. "It goes back to those fundamental questions."

'Sacrifice' proved to be a particularly emotional episode to make for the actors involved with Billy Keikeya's death scene. "We shot that as the final scene of that episode, at the end of the day," Kandyse McClure recalls. "It was really difficult for us to see Paul go. I felt he was prematurely ripped from the fold. I really was crying, both on and off camera."

Fortunately, Campbell himself did his best to keep his colleagues smiling during his final moments on the *Battlestar Galactica* set. "When I finished my last scene, I actually had the First

SURVEILLANCE: ADDITIONAL

If Billy Keikeya had remained a part of *Battlestar Galactica*, Moore planned to develop the character's political rise. "We were going to continue the Billy-Laura storyline," he explains. "The idea was that Laura was going to start grooming Billy to be a politician or to take some position of authority within the fleet. We'd said in 'Home' that Laura had told Adama she thought Billy would be President one day, so he was going to be aimed in that direction. But we didn't have any specific plans beyond that."

Above: Dualla watches over Lee.

AD [assistant director] announce 'That's a career wrap for Paul Campbell' as a joke," he reveals with a laugh. "I had a nice last day on the show. Everyone wished me luck. Jamie and Kandyse and David Eick and Harvey Frand were all around, and Eddie hung around eight hours after he was supposed to go home just to say goodbye, which was nice."

By the time of its completion, Moore viewed 'Sacrifice' as an episode that didn't quite fulfill its potential, despite its emotional scenes involving Billy's death. But Campbell himself has no real complaints about the episode and feels it does provide a fitting swansong for his character. "I was happy with Billy's demise in 'Sacrifice'," states Campbell. "Whenever a character leaves a show, they try their best to make the episode about them and try to give them the best send-off they can. In that sense the episode was great. We ended up going a few places with the Billy/Dualla relationship that I think were a little too quick for the drama — I thought the engagement was premature. But I loved the rest of it, which was about Billy becoming a man and standing up and fighting.

"At the same time, I did think to myself, 'If the producers had given me an episode like this at the beginning of the season, I might have signed up for more!'" he adds with a laugh. "It was unfortunate that the first really great episode for Billy was the one he died in. But it made good television." ∎

[THE CAPTAIN'S HAND]

WRITER: Jeff Vlaming
DIRECTOR:
Sergio Mimica-Gezzan

GUEST CAST: John Heard (Commander Barry Garner), Amber Rothwell (Rya Kibby), Patricia Idlette (Sarah Porter), Rekha Sharma (Tory Foster), Stephanie von Pfetten (Captain Marcia 'Showboat' Case), Brad Dryborough (Hoshi), Kavan Smith (Lt Richard 'Buster' Baier), Alisen Down (Jean Barolay), Christina Schild (Playa), Christian Tessier (Tucker 'Duck' Clellan), Kimani Ray Smith (Pegasus Sergeant), Kurt Max Runte (Ensign Charles Bellamy), James Bell (Lt Steve 'Red Devil' Fleer), Tammy Hui (ECO Lyla 'Shark' Ellway), Aaron Pearl (Ensign Abel Thornton)

"I am forced to take command of this vessel under Federal regulations and place you under arrest..."
— Major Adama, to Commander Barry Garner

Lee Adama is promoted to the rank of Major and temporarily appointed as the Executive Officer of the *Pegasus*. Lee's new Commander on the *Pegasus* is Barry Garner, the Battlestar's former Engine Chief. On assuming his post, Major Adama is informed that two of the *Pegasus*' Raptors mysteriously went missing while investigating a distress signal. Lee, Kara Thrace and Admiral Adama all suspect the Raptors have fallen victim to a Cylon trap, but Commander Garner disobeys Admiral Adama's orders and sends the *Pegasus* in pursuit of the missing ships. When Lee challenges Garner's authority, he is relieved of duty.

After locating the Raptors, the *Pegasus* crew discover their missing colleagues are dead and the Battlestar is immediately attacked by three Cylon Basestars. As the *Pegasus* takes heavy damage, Garner gives his life conducting vital engineering repairs that enable Major Adama to take the *Pegasus* to safety. Lee is later appointed as the Battlestar's new Commander by his father.

Back on the *Galactica*, a pregnant teenager's desire for an abortion becomes a focal point in the Presidential election campaign. After the fleet's pro-life Gemenon faction objects to the termination, President Roslin reluctantly agrees to make abortion illegal. But Roslin's decision prompts Gaius Baltar to launch his own surprise bid for the Presidency.

The primary plotline of 'The Captain's Hand' was largely driven by Ronald D. Moore's decision to appoint Lee Adama as the *Pegasus*' commanding officer. "That idea came from a lot of different discussions we had about Lee and the *Pegasus*," Moore explains. "We were looking for something for Lee to do beyond being the *Galactica*'s CAG, and as we started getting into the idea of using the *Pegasus* more, we realized that putting one of

Above: 'The Captain's Hand' was conceived as the episode that would mark Lee Adama's appointment as the *Pegasus'* new commanding officer.

our characters over there on an ongoing basis was a way of keeping the *Pegasus* in the story all the time. We knew that the *Pegasus* would have extra meaning to the show and the viewers if one of the main characters was commanding it.

"When we first asked ourselves who could be the Commander of *Pegasus*, we all knew it wasn't going to be Tigh," he continues. "Tigh had said outright he didn't want a command of his own and we'd seen him in command, so it didn't seem like the best idea. After that the next candidate was Lee, and we were looking for something for Lee to do anyway. So it was a nice fit."

'The Captain's Hand' was scripted by freelance scribe Jeff Vlaming. A veteran TV writer/producer whose many credits include *The X-Files*, *Northern Exposure* and *Xena: Warrior Princess*, Vlaming had previously penned the season one *Battlestar Galactica* installments 'Litmus' and 'Tigh Me Up, Tigh Me Down', and was invited to script his third episode of the series when he visited Moore at Universal's Hollywood lot. "I walked into Ron's office and he said, 'We were just trying to call you! We wanted to ask if you would like to write an episode'," Vlaming recalls. "I instantly said, 'Of course! Yes, I'd love to.' *Battlestar Galactica* is such an amazing show — it's such a superb character-driven drama — and Ron and the writers are second to none, so I didn't have to give it much thought.

"When I went in to meet with Ron and the writers about the episode, they had a rough idea of what they wanted to do with the *Pegasus* storyline. They said they wanted to do something like the Humphrey Bogart movie *The Caine Mutiny* — they wanted to do an episode about an incompetent captain who finds himself in over his head in a crisis situation."

While the basic premise of 'The Captain's Hand' remained constant from the episode's conception to its completion, various aspects of the episode's primary plotline changed during its development. In early versions of the storyline, Lee clashed with the *Pegasus'* Commander over his determination to be liked by his crew and obvious unwillingness to enforce military discipline on the Battlestar. Vlaming's script also initially saw Lee having to sacrifice the lives of several Viper pilots to save the *Pegasus*, while his commanding officer survived the crisis. The original storyline concluded with Lee being appointed as the *Pegasus'* permanent Commander at the suggestion of his predecessor. In a further change from the original storyline, the *Pegasus* Commander was initially called Trammel, until he was renamed Garner for legal clearance reasons.

"In the original four drafts I did, the Commander was really likeable — Lee really liked the guy," Vlaming explains. "Trammel, as he was then called, wanted everyone to be his friend and he was so different from Lee's father that Lee really took to the guy. But we found that within the constraints of a forty-two-minute episode, we didn't have the time to build to a big transformation where Trammel changes as he's faced with the duplicitous behavior of his crew. So in the finished episode it's clear from the start he's in way over his head."

"After I turned in my last draft, Lee's trajectory also changed," he notes. "In the earlier drafts, he had to sacrifice some pilots to escape. I thought that would have been a very powerful first step for him to take into being a Commander."

The finished version of 'The Captain's Hand' sees Lee fighting to take command of the *Pegasus* from Garner at one point, in a scene inspired by the 1995 submarine movie *Crimson Tide*. It also has Garner sacrificing himself to save the *Pegasus* during the episode's climax. Garner's last stand was devised to be light years away from the high-tech engineering scenes normally seen on sci-fi shows. "I didn't want to do the type of thing you normally see on *Star Trek*," explains Moore. "I wanted it to be visceral and immediate and very simple, with Garner just trying to turn a valve."

'The Captain's Hand' was the fourth hour of *Battlestar Galactica* to be directed by Sergio Mimica-Gezzan. Like 'Resurrection Ship, Part II' and 'Black Market', it proved to be a key installment of season two for Jamie Bamber. "I really enjoyed that episode," he says. "It went through a few rewrites and wasn't as dark as it was initially going to be, but it was still important for my character. I found myself promoted from Captain to Major to Commander, all in the same episode!"

Bamber shares the bulk of his screen time in 'The Captain's Hand' with John Heard, a veteran character actor whose credits include *Big*, *The Sopranos* and *Home Alone*. "I thought we were lucky to get him to play such a pivotal role in our show," says David Eick of Heard's performance as Commander Garner. "He's a very recognizable character actor, and he did a great job for us."

The B-plot of 'The Captain's Hand' sees Laura Roslin becoming embroiled in a political dilemma involving a young woman's desire to have an abortion. This scenario was originally discussed by the show's writing staff during the development of season one and had its origins in ideas suggested by the show's Series Bible.

"I always thought it would be interesting to explore how Roslin would balance the issue of people's rights to birth control and abortion with the need for people to have babies, to ensure the survival of the species," Moore explains. "By doing that storyline near the end of season two, it allowed us to show Laura's decision to play the religious card [earlier in the season] coming back to haunt her. And, of course, it was a great way to set up the idea of Baltar running for President.

Above: Lee Adama discusses his new assignment with Kara Thrace.

"The thing I like about the storyline is that we didn't do the usual cop-out ending," Moore notes. "Rya has her abortion. It's a very dramatic decision, and it's true to the reality of the situation."

"Ron and the writers had a clear idea of the B-story by the time I started working on the episode," Vlaming adds. "It came out pretty much exactly how I wrote it."

The episode's B-plot also serves to introduce Roslin's new assistant, Tory Foster. "We wanted Tory to be very different from Billy," says Eick of Rekha Sharma's character. "She's really in Laura's face, and she's more of a foil for her."

At one point in 'The Captain's Hand', Roslin reluctantly tells Sarah Porter that she will have her "pound of flesh". This line is a reference to Shakespeare's *The Merchant of Venice*. "It could be argued that line doesn't belong on *Battlestar Galactica*," Moore concedes. "I played with variations on it, but I just couldn't think of a better phrase."

As the episode that launches Gaius Baltar on the road to the Presidency and also marks the beginning of Lee Adama's command of the *Pegasus*, 'The Captain's Hand' would ultimately be regarded by Moore as an important installment of *Battlestar Galactica*'s second season. "'The Captain's Hand' really shakes up the structure of the show," he explains. "It brings some changes for the characters, which I think is believable and again demonstrates we're not a formulaic television series. It also raises some really interesting possibilities for the show's future." ∎

[DOWNLOADED]

WRITERS: Bradley Thompson & David Weddle
DIRECTOR: Jeff Woolnough

GUEST CAST: Lucy Lawless (D'Anna Biers), Matthew Bennett (Aaron Doral), Rekha Sharma (Tory Foster), Kerry Norton (Paramedic Layne Ishay), Erica Cerra (Maya), Alisen Down (Jean Barolay)

"Our people need a new beginning..." — Caprica Six

Following her death during the Cylon assault on Caprica, the Number Six assigned to seduce Gaius Baltar awakens among the Cylons, her consciousness downloaded into a new body. 'Caprica Six' is disturbed by her involvement in the holocaust and secretly haunted by visions of Baltar.

Half a year later, Caprica Six is asked to spend time with another of the Cylons' "war heroes", the Number Eight who lived on the *Galactica* as Lieutenant Sharon 'Boomer' Valerii. Caprica Six learns that 'Boomer Eight' is still struggling to come to terms with her nature and that the Cylons are thinking of "boxing" her — placing her consciousness in cold storage.

After narrowly surviving a resistance attack, Boomer Eight and Caprica Six stop a Number Three/D'Anna Biers Cylon from killing Kara Thrace's lover, Samuel Anders. They then agree to try to convince the Cylons to reevaluate their current strategy and recent decisions.

Far from Caprica, the Sharon aboard the *Galactica* prematurely gives birth to Hera, the human-Cylon child she conceived with Helo. As the infant fights for life, President Roslin decides that the Cylons cannot learn of her existence and orders the baby to be secretly adopted by a trustworthy young woman, Maya. Helo and Sharon are then told of their baby's death...

SURVEILLANCE: ADDITIONAL

Sharon's baby was named Hera following a discussion between Bradley Thompson and David Weddle. "We have Homer's *The Iliad* and *The Odyssey* on our bookshelf in the office — the Robert Fagles translations — and we constantly thumb through them for ancient Greek names of everything from people to towns," Weddle explains. "In that instance, it was Brad who first suggested the name Hera."

'Downloaded' was borne of Ronald D. Moore's desire to make a *Battlestar Galactica* episode that told a story from the Cylons' point of view. Its production followed the development of a completely different Cylon-centric episode entitled 'The Raid', which involved the Cylon equivalent of the Nazis' 1942 Wannsee conference and saw the *Galactica* crew infiltrating a Cylon space station to steal information about Earth. 'The Raid' was initially scripted by Carla Robinson and then worked on by several other members of the show's writing staff, but the episode was ultimately abandoned.

"We struggled with that storyline and just couldn't get it to work," Moore reveals. "But we were in love with the notion of doing a Cylon story and were determined to find a way of doing it. We all felt doing a Cylon episode would add a new dimension to how we viewed the Cylons — the characters we have been regarding as the enemy — and add an extra layer of complexity to the show."

Following the scrapping of 'The Raid', Bradley Thompson and David Weddle were invited to develop their idea for a Cylon episode. Their concept picked up the adventures of the Boomer Sharon and Caprica Six, after their last appearances in 'Resistance' and the opening part of the miniseries respectively.

"We were dying to see what happened to Caprica Six and Boomer," explains Thompson, "and it occurred to us that their experiences with love had probably messed up their chances for seamless reintegration into Cylon society. We also liked the idea that the Cylons would try and get Six, who had her own problems with love, to try and sort Boomer out."

To give Boomer's struggle to reintegrate into Cylon society added drama, 'Downloaded' made the character face what Thompson describes as "the perfect horror": the threat of being "boxed"; spending eternity permanently incarcerated, with no chance of parole or release by death. The writers also developed an idea Toni Graphia first suggested while working on 'The Raid' into a key element of the episode. "Toni had long advocated that Caprica Six could have a Baltar in her head as a manifestation of her guilt, just as he has her in his head," Weddle reveals. "Ron loved the idea, so that was also incorporated into the show."

With Boomer and Six's character arcs for the episode in place, the writers then sought a scenario that would put the episode's Cylon characters into direct conflict with humans.

Above: Karl Agathon faces the apparent death of his daughter in the episode's moving B-plot.

They found that scenario with Anders' destruction of a coffee shop full of civilian Cylons, using a cigarette bomb featured in a real-life explosives handbook. "We loved the idea because it frakked with all our feelings of good guys and bad guys, and that's one of the strengths of the series," says Thompson. "Anders makes a deliberate attack on a non-military target to create fear — which means it's an act of terrorism. But if our good guys are terrorists, how can we root for them?"

As the director of 'Downloaded', *Battlestar Galactica* veteran Jeff Woolnough was required to reveal a lot about Cylon society in a manner that, somehow, didn't demystify it. Woolnough discussed this issue extensively with the show's writers and producers throughout shooting, some of which took place at Vancouver's Waterfall Building. "One of the fun things that Ron and David Eick came up with is that in places like the coffee shop, most Cylons don't generally speak," Thompson notes. "When Jeff Woolnough staged the scene without background chatting, it definitely felt weird."

'Downloaded' marked Lucy Lawless' second appearance as Number Three, otherwise known as D'Anna Biers. "What was great about that episode was that it required me to create a sense of underlying menace," says Lawless. "D'Anna is claiming she wants to be a friend to Sharon and Six, but instinctively you don't quite trust her."

"Lucy came up with great ideas for depicting D'Anna in that episode," Thompson adds. "It was her idea to do most of the show as a 'mumsy' D'Anna, which beautifully counterpoints the other actors' fear of her."

Lawless' appreciation of 'Downloaded' was shared by Tricia Helfer, Grace Park and James Callis, all of whom enjoyed the episode's unusual premise. "I thought it was a fun episode for the audience and for us," Helfer explains. "It was fascinating to see the original Six and Boomer again and follow their struggle, and it was great to work with Grace and Lucy. And I thought Six having Baltar inside her head was a very interesting idea."

Six's interaction with her imaginary Baltar was supported by some striking musical cues devised by Bear McCreary. "For the sequences where Number Six sees visions of Baltar in her head, the score features snippets of the Number Six theme literally turned backwards," he reveals. "This helps augment their role reversal."

The multiple Cylons seen in 'Downloaded' were realized thanks to the use of motion control. The visual effects department was also responsible for the brief shot of the Cylon

Centurion planting a tree on Caprica, which was an addition to the script from Moore.

"The motion control stuff was fun to do," says Matthew Bennett, whose character Aaron Doral received the Cylon designation Number Five in the episode. "I got to do things like serve myself coffee in the café! Things like that really help to build the Cylon world and flesh it out."

Moore was aware that many viewers expected 'Downloaded' to reveal the identities of all twelve humanoid-appearing Cylons, but deliberately decided against the idea as it would have prevented him from surprising the audience later on. Instead, it was agreed early in the development of the episode that it would only feature multiple models of Three, Five, Six and Eight (though the treacherous Simon from 'The Farm' can be glimpsed briefly in a scene, when he is played not by Rick Worthy but by a look-alike).

'Downloaded' combines the Cylon storyline with a B-plot involving the birth of Sharon's half-human, half-Cylon baby Hera and President Roslin's attempts to protect her from being discovered by the Cylons. Hera's sudden arrival in this episode, rather than the season finale, represented another attempt to surprise the audience.

"We were thrilled that we got to write the birth of Sharon's baby since we had been involved in the development of that storyline since the beginning of the series," says Weddle. "It was David Eick's idea that Laura would kidnap the baby. At first I resisted this as I wasn't sure it would work, but once we got in there and began writing it we realized what a stroke of genius it was and how this opened all kinds of doors for the ongoing saga of the baby.

"Grace's performance in that episode was incredible," he adds. "When Sharon wailed at the death of her child, I was wiping tears from my eyes on the set."

Hera's arrival proved similarly memorable for Donnelly Rhodes (Dr Cottle). "The art department did a great job of creating a baby for that episode," he recalls. "It was pretty realistic; it looked like a real baby. I had to manipulate it for certain scenes, which was an interesting experience."

The episode's B-plot culminates in Karl Agathon and Chief Tyrol releasing what they believe to be the baby's ashes into space. "That was a very touching moment," Thompson notes. "It resonated hauntingly with my own experience watching someone's ashes vanish into the ocean."

Thanks to its blend of innovative storytelling and poignant drama, 'Downloaded' emerged as one of season two's most intriguing and memorable installments. It would also pave the way for further Cylon-centric storylines.

"We were exceptionally happy with the way the episode came out," states Thompson. "This episode opened the door to the Cylon world and you can expect to see much more of it as the show progresses." ■

 SURVEILLANCE: ADDITIONAL

'Downloaded' originally contained a sub-plot about an attempt to kidnap Sharon's baby involving Baltar, the Gina Six and D'Anna Biers. Their scheme was set to be thwarted by President Roslin, who was going to use D'Anna's request to make a report about Hera as a way of revealing the baby's death to the fleet. "We had to drop that storyline because there was too much going on already and too many Cylons," states Moore.

The episode was also initially set to feature a scene at the ruins of Baltar's house on Caprica, but this had to be dropped for budgetary and scheduling reasons.

[LAY DOWN YOUR BURDENS PART I]

WRITER: Ronald D. Moore
DIRECTOR: Michael Rymer

GUEST CAST: Dean Stockwell (Brother Cavil), Rekha Sharma (Tory Foster), Alisen Down (Jean Barolay), David Kaye (James McManus), Colin Lawrence (Hamish 'Skulls' McCall)

> "We need an issue. Something to set us apart from Roslin. Something to put her clearly on the wrong side of a major issue people care passionately about. This is it: permanent settlement on this planet."
> — Tom Zarek, to Baltar

As Laura Roslin emerges as firm favorite to win the upcoming Presidential election, Lieutenant Kara Thrace leads a high-risk search-and-rescue mission back to Caprica. During the first in a series of FTL Jumps, a Raptor is separated from the rest of the rescue party and finds itself in the vicinity of a nebula that cloaks a planet capable of supporting human life.

After learning of the Raptor crew's discovery, Tom Zarek suggests that Gaius Baltar could gain support by expressing his belief in permanent settlement on the planet. Baltar makes this idea the centerpiece of his campaign and enjoys a rapid increase in popularity.

Meanwhile, Chief Tyrol is wracked with guilt after he accidentally assaults Cally when she wakes him from a recurring nightmare. Tyrol enlists the counsel of Brother Cavil, who suggests the Chief has been dreaming of killing himself because he fears he is a Cylon.

Arriving on Caprica, Kara and her team locate the resistance, including Samuel Anders. But Kara's passionate reunion with Anders is short-lived, as their group quickly find themselves outgunned and cornered by the Cylons...

Opposite: Tom Zarek and Number Six come up with an idea that will transform Gaius Baltar's Presidential campaign in 'Lay Down Your Burdens, Part I'.

SURVEILLANCE: ADDITIONAL

Ronald D. Moore was never concerned about the apparent similarity between the plotlines of 'Lay Down Your Burdens' and season one's finale 'Kobol's Last Gleaming', which also involved the *Galactica*'s discovery of a planet. "We did talk about that," he acknowledges, "but the big distinction was that there never really was any question of settling on Kobol, as the Cylons were in orbit as soon as our characters discovered it. The discovery of Kobol was a big thing for the characters' back-story, but they never were going to settle there."

"The premise for 'Lay Down Your Burdens' came naturally from all the plotlines we'd been developing during the past two years of the show," says Ronald D. Moore of season two's two-part finale. "We had been promising the audience a Presidential election ever since 'Bastille Day' in season one and we repeatedly talked about doing it in season two. But we weren't sure how to do it, because elections aren't normally very dramatic in TV shows and films — they're all about speechmaking and banners. We knew we had to find an interesting issue for the election to center on.

"As soon as we came up with the idea of finding a habitable planet, I realized that was the thing the election should center on," he reveals. "I wanted the question of whether the fleet should settle on the planet to be the defining issue of the election, and the issue that costs Laura Roslin the election, because without it she would have won.

"I knew Laura would have to lose the election, because otherwise there would be little point telling an election story. How interesting would it be if Laura had just won the election? So we started talking about Tom Zarek or Baltar winning the election, and we started gravitating towards Baltar's direction very quickly."

The season finale's other main plotline also represented the culmination of earlier events in the series. "As soon as we did 'The Farm', we knew we were going to have to go back to Caprica," explains Moore. "From the moment Kara committed herself to Anders and gave him the dog-tags and said, 'I'm going to be back', it was a given we were going to have to come back and do something with that story. We used the idea that the characters had found a way to link the Cylon Heavy Raider's systems to the Raptor as the means of their return."

An additional plot strand of 'Lay Down Your Burdens, Part I' was inspired by a suggestion from David Eick, who wanted to see Chief Tyrol facing a "psychotic meltdown" as a result of the events of the past season. Moore came up with the idea of Tyrol's "shocking" attack on Cally, which originally took place off-screen, until Eick pointed out it would be much

Above: Ronald D. Moore always knew that *Battlestar Galactica*'s first Presidential election storyline would end in a dramatic defeat for Roslin.

more dramatic to show it. The Tyrol sub-plot also served to set up his partnering with a new love interest, Cally.

"I really wanted to bring as many issues to the table as I possibly could for the finale," Moore notes. "We also follow up things like the Helo, Sharon and the baby storyline. I wanted the finale to touch the lives of all the different characters and show how they're all involved in the same world."

Moore decided to personally script the opening part of the season finale, but would assign the storyline of the conclusion to writers Mark Verheiden and Anne Cofell Saunders. "I really like doing the set-up and the character stuff of a Part I," he explains. "Part IIs are normally about resolutions and tying things up."

Battlestar Galactica's principal director, Michael Rymer, returned to the show to helm both parts of 'Lay Down Your Burdens'. "What

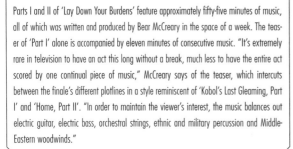

SURVEILLANCE: ADDITIONAL

Parts I and II of 'Lay Down Your Burdens' feature approximately fifty-five minutes of music, all of which was written and produced by Bear McCreary in the space of a week. The teaser of 'Part I' alone is accompanied by eleven minutes of consecutive music. "It's extremely rare in television to have an act this long without a break, much less to have the entire act scored by one continual piece of music," McCreary says of the teaser, which intercuts between the finale's different plotlines in a style reminiscent of 'Kobol's Last Gleaming, Part I' and 'Home, Part II'. "In order to maintain the viewer's interest, the music balances out electric guitar, electric bass, orchestral strings, ethnic and military percussion and Middle-Eastern woodwinds."

I really loved about doing those two episodes was that they're driven by character and relationships, sexuality, psychology and politics," he says. "There's a good whack of action — I thought the fire-fight in the forest was pretty good — but it's more about other things."

Another aspect of the finale that excited Rymer was the casting of screen legend Dean Stockwell as Brother Cavil. Amusingly, Stockwell hadn't seen a single episode of the new *Battlestar Galactica* prior to working on the show and had agreed to guest star purely on the strength of the finale's script.

"My agent had been talking to the people on the show for a while and when this part came up I was happy to do it," says Stockwell, whose many screen credits include *Blue Velvet*, *Quantum Leap* and *Dune*. "The script was well written and it was a very interesting role, and I thought I could do a good job on it.

"I hadn't seen the show when I did those episodes, so it was a bit of a challenge," he admits. "I found myself relying almost one hundred per cent on my hunches and intuition. But everyone seemed to agree my approach was a good one. The cast and crew were terrific, and Michael Rymer was very sweet."

Above: Baltar quickly emerged in the writers' room as the most interesting character who could become the new President of the Twelve Colonies of Kobol.

Scripting Brother Cavil's interaction with Chief Tyrol proved interesting for Moore, who enjoyed exploring the relationship between a priest who has lost his faith and the Lords of Kobol-fearing son of a Colonial cleric. Exploring this relationship was also memorable for Aaron Douglas. "I had some great scenes with Dean Stockwell," he says. "He's a very cool guy."

While counseling Tyrol, Brother Cavil quips that the Chief can't be a Cylon because he hasn't seen him at any of their meetings. "That was a call-back to a line in the miniseries," Moore notes, "where Number Six says that she doesn't remember seeing Aaron Doral at any of the Cylon parties."

Both the closing moments of 'Lay Down Your Burdens, Part I' and the opening moments of the second episode are driven by Kara Thrace's search-and-rescue mission to Caprica. "I loved shooting the SWAT stuff for those episodes," says Katee Sackhoff. "It was hard work — those packs were really heavy — but it was a lot of fun firing my weapons while doing these dramatic scenes.

"What was really great about it was my mom was on set on one of the days we did a lot of that stuff," she continues, "and our military advisor told her afterwards that I was more capable than most of the guys he went to war with! I was like, 'Wow. I've truly arrived as Starbuck!'" ■

[LAY DOWN YOUR BURDENS PART II]

WRITERS: Anne Cofell Saunders & Mark Verheiden
DIRECTOR: Michael Rymer

GUEST CAST: Dean Stockwell (Brother Cavil), Callum Keith Rennie (Leoben), Matthew Bennett (Aaron Doral), Rekha Sharma (Tory Foster), Alisen Down (Jean Barolay), Erica Cerra (Maya), Winston Rekert (Priest), David Kaye (James McManus)

> "On behalf of the people of the Twelve Colonies, I surrender."
> — President Baltar, to the Cylons

After the Cylons mysteriously halt their attack on the Caprica resistance movement, Kara Thrace takes Anders and the other survivors back to the *Galactica*. Once there, Brother Cavil announces himself as a Cylon and reveals that his people have adopted a new strategy. Cavil tells Admiral Adama and President Roslin that models of Number Six and Number Eight have convinced the Cylons to stop trying to annihilate humanity and pursue other plans.

With the Presidential election approaching, Roslin realizes that Baltar's support for the colonization of the planet dubbed New Caprica is increasingly turning the tide in his favor. She privately asks him to put the issue aside until after the election, but Baltar only takes that as a sign that he is winning the Presidential race. Roslin also tells Baltar she can remember seeing him with Number Six on Caprica shortly before the Cylon attack, but he refuses to discuss the matter with her.

When the votes are finally counted, Roslin initially seems to have won the Presidential election — until Gaeta realizes the ballot has been rigged by Roslin and her campaign manager, with the help of Colonel Tigh. Faced with a choice between denying the will of the people and allowing a man they suspect is a Cylon collaborator to become President, Roslin and Adama agree they cannot stop Baltar from taking his elected position.

As President Baltar is sworn in, his Cylon lover Gina destroys *Cloud Nine* with her nuclear bomb. Following the tragedy, Baltar orders the colonization of New Caprica.

One year later, the *Pegasus* is orbiting New Caprica with the *Galactica* when it detects the approach of a Cylon fleet that has been drawn to the area by traces of the nuclear explosion detonated by Gina. Realizing they are hopelessly outnumbered, Commander Lee Adama advises Admiral Adama that they should Jump away. The Admiral reluctantly agrees with his son and the Battlestars Jump to safety, not before Admiral Adama vows to return.

On New Caprica, President Gaius Baltar offers his surrender to the Cylons on behalf of all the Colonists. As the Cylons begin their occupation of New Caprica, Kara Thrace tells Chief Tyrol and Cally their fight has only just begun…

SURVEILLANCE: ADDITIONAL

'Lay Down Your Burdens, Part II' was initially scripted and shot as a standard, sixty-minute installment of *Battlestar Galactica*. But it was expanded into a ninety-minute episode after it became clear that there were too many story developments and character moments to fit into a sixty-minute time slot. Prior to its extension, an early cut of the episode simply ended with Baltar becoming President and also removed the moment in which Laura confronts Baltar about his involvement with Number Six.

'Lay Down Your Burdens, Part II' allowed Ronald D. Moore to fulfill a long-time ambition. "I'd been interested in the concept of doing a time jump like that in a series for quite a while," says Moore of the season two finale's year-skipping narrative. "When I was working on *Carnivale* I was interested in jumping back and doing a whole season that was set completely in the past and then jumping forward again. I was interested in playing with timeframes, because it's something TV is typically reluctant to do.

"So as we were talking about the specifics of 'Lay Down Your Burdens, Part II', I knew that a time jump would be a way of giving the decision to go down to New Caprica meaning. I figured it would allow us to see what it would be like if they had settled down and had Baltar as a President, in a way that didn't change the show so much that it effectively became a different series entirely. If we had just followed that year on New Caprica it would have taken the Cylons and the quest for Earth out of the show for a year, and the show wouldn't have been *Battlestar Galactica*.

"I always knew the finale was a risk," he admits. "But this show is about risks, as opposed to playing safe and doing things the way they're always done in science fiction shows and television in general."

The one-year time jump wasn't the only big surprise delivered by season two's closing episode, though. 'Lay Down Your Burdens, Part II' also sees Laura Roslin becoming involved in a plot to prevent Baltar from taking his place as the rightfully elected President of the Twelve Colonies of Kobol. This plot development convinced Moore and David Eick to pursue the election storyline, as they felt it gave the event an added element of interest.

"I thought Laura's attempt to steal the election would allow us to explore what it means to live in a democratic society and ask how far are you willing to stand behind that idea," Moore explains. "Laura would do anything she could to keep Baltar — a man she believes is a Cylon collaborator — out of power, but I also felt she couldn't really break a fundamental idea about what it means to live in a democracy.

"Some people might argue that they should steal the election anyway," he acknowledges. "But it seems important that even in a dark show like this, our two main characters wouldn't steal the election. They wouldn't cross that line and sell their souls."

"The election and Roslin's decision to cheat to keep Baltar from winning was my favorite aspect of the episode," adds Mark Verheiden, who scripted 'Lay Down Your Burdens, Part II' with Anne Cofell Saunders. "Laura is forced to do the wrong thing for the greater good, only to have the whole mess explode in her face. It's a wonderful character point and Mary McDonnell is so good at showing the President's torment."

Two other surprises contained in 'Lay Down Your Burdens, Part II' concern the Cylons' change of plan and Brother Cavil's exposure as a Cylon. The former idea was designed to set the scene for some intriguing developments planned for season three, while the latter provided the basis of a memorable scene in which two Brother Cavils interact with each other in jail, thanks to stop motion visual effects. "I loved shooting that scene," says Dean Stockwell. "It was very interesting to 'act' with myself. I'd never done anything quite like that before."

"I thought Dean Stockwell was amazing in that scene," Moore adds. "He's acting like there really are two of them. He's superb at it."

Before the settlement of New Caprica, Gina sacrifices herself in a nuclear explosion that later alerts the Cylons to the planet's location. Gina's final acts include a farewell to Baltar. "We shot a very explicit love scene between Gina and Baltar which contained much more [footage] than I could ever use," Rymer notes. "But I needed to do that to make the glimpses of the love scene as powerful as they are."

Following Baltar's inauguration, the action skips forward a year in the middle of an act, just as Moore had always planned. The episode then wastes no time in establishing the various characters' new positions and roles in life. "We show that these people and their relationships have moved on in the year," Moore says. "We make it clear that it really has happened — it's a not a dream or anything else like that — and we show that the characters have developed in some really interesting ways."

To ensure that New Caprica emerged as a 'desert-like environment' that was

SURVEILLANCE: ADDITIONAL

The closing moments of 'Lay Down Your Burdens, Part II' see Chief Tyrol giving a speech which was based on a real-life public address given by the late civil rights activist Mario Savio in 1964. "It's a speech that's very special to me," says David Eick. "Mario Savio's widow gave us permission to paraphrase it, and she liked the way we did it."

distinct from other planets previously featured on *Battlestar Galactica*, the series' makers decided not to shoot the episode's exterior scenes in any of the show's regular Vancouver locations. After considering shooting in a variety of far-away locations including Pitcairn, British Columbia, the show's makers ultimately settled on an area in relatively nearby Richmond. "There was a giant sand dune there that had been used by other productions in the past," Harvey Frand points out, "so we made that work for us."

While shooting the New Caprica exterior scenes, Eick suggested that Rymer used the classic Western movie *McCabe and Mrs Miller* as a source of inspiration for the planet's look. Rymer's footage was subsequently augmented by visual effects.

"I think the location turned out exceptionally well," says Moore. "I think it's the best alien settlement I've ever been involved with, and that includes all my years on *Star Trek*."

After a brief nod to Hera's whereabouts and a glimpse of the cradle featured in Baltar's visions on Kobol, 'Lay Down Your Burdens, Part II' concludes with a final shock, as Cylon Centurions invade New Caprica. This sequence was scripted to resemble the Nazis marching into Paris in 1940 and presented a major challenge for the show's visual effects department.

Above: The closing moments of season two bring some startling changes for many of the show's characters.

"That shot concerned all of us," explains Gary Hutzel. "We felt it could go either way: it could either be great or silly. When we looked at an early version of the scene, it felt a little preposterous; I think someone joked, 'The Cylon circus is in town!' But we were able to make it work and it came together quite nicely in the end."

The bulk of principal photography on season two's finale was completed by Friday 2 December 2005, although a further five days of second unit shooting followed. By the time the season had wrapped, it was clear that the 'Lay Down Your Burdens' two-parter represented a remarkable end to an electrifying season.

"We ended season one shooting Adama and said we didn't want to try to top ourselves with the season two finale," Moore notes. "But the season two finale is even bigger. It's bigger conceptually."

"I'm really proud of the finale because it's dramatic, it's risky and it pushes viewers' preconceptions of what the show is," he declares. "You think anything is possible at the end — and that's a great thing to do on a television show." ■

[THE CHARACTERS]

"*Battlestar Galactica*'s characters are living, breathing people with all the emotional complexity and contradictions present in quality dramas like *The West Wing* or *The Sopranos...*" **— Ronald D. Moore**

[WILLIAM ADAMA]

"It's not enough to survive. One has to be worthy of surviving."

Edward James Olmos feels that *Battlestar Galactica*'s second season gave William Adama a new lease of life — in more ways than one. "I thought my character's arc for season two was very interesting," says Olmos. "It begins with Adama coming back from the dead, after dying twice on the operating table. That experience has a lasting effect on him, and we explore that over the course of season two.

"When Adama returns to duty in episode five ['The Farm'], you have a whole new Adama standing in front of his crew," he notes. "He's been sensitized and has become more emotional and philosophical. He's started questioning his mortality and his decisions and his relationships, and has also begun to feel much more for everything and everyone that's around him. That makes Adama stronger as a human being, because he becomes much more intuitive about hubhhgjgjhgjhgens him as a leader in a time of war. He's no longer as quick to make harsh decisions, because he's concerned about the people he's sending out to battle.

"That was a great direction to take the character in," Olmos adds. "That arc showed a different side of Adama and gave him something new to work for — he has to find a way to come back and regain his strength."

Season two also brought some radical changes for Adama's relationships with many of the people around him, most notably Laura Roslin. The season's opening civil war story arc sees Adama reaching a new understanding with his former rival.

"Adama grows to understand and admire Roslin and what she's going through in the early part of season two," Olmos explains. "He becomes very emotional as he sees her approaching death. They develop a strong friendship, but their relationship is strained again at the end of the season by her attempt to rig the election.

"It was good to explore that relationship with Mary," he continues, "and it gave us some very memorable scenes. The scenes where Roslin is on her deathbed were extremely powerful and the moment where Adama is promoted to Admiral was very emotional. That was a life-changing moment for him."

Another key change for Adama concerned his relationship with Sharon Valerii. Season two saw Adama struggling to come to terms with Sharon's betrayal and her exposure as a Cylon. "Adama's relationship with Sharon was a fascinating part of season two," says Olmos. "It's a really complex and conflicted love/hate relationship. Sharon was like a daughter to Adama — she loved him dearly — and so he finds it hard to come to terms with the idea she is a Cylon. He also doesn't know how far he can trust her — if at all."

Clearly, *Battlestar Galactica*'s second season wasn't short of dramatic developments for William Adama. It also provided Olmos with plenty of acting challenges, all of which were welcomed by the veteran film and TV star.

"I've got to tell you I'm really enjoying playing this character," Olmos states. "I'm *living* the character. I think we're all doing that. We're being honest with the moment and

making it connect. It's extraordinary. The scenes come alive every single time. It's great ensemble work.

"I so enjoyed working with everyone in season two. I find it beautiful to work with Mary and Michael Hogan and all the young actors, and all the different guest stars we had coming on the show in season two were great. Michelle Forbes is a very, very strong actress and I think she was perfect for the role of Admiral Cain. Lucy Lawless was also exceptional and, at the end of the season, Dean Stockwell was just magnificent. I remember working with him on *Miami Vice* — I actually directed him in his first appearance on the show — and he's a great, great actor.

"Every scene we did in season two was memorable to me. I think the only thing I didn't particularly enjoy were the scenes where Adama is lying down in the hospital — being inactive like that is very difficult and it's not something I'd like to do again. But, overall, it has been incredible."

After directing the first-season *Battlestar Galactica* installment 'Tigh Me Up, Tigh Me Down', Olmos initially looked set to helm an episode of season two. But his work as the director of the HBO movie *Walkout* prevented him from spending any time in the director's chair during the show's second year. "I had hoped to direct an episode in season two," Olmos confirms, "but I was too busy acting in the show and directing *Walkout*. We shot the movie in the mid-season production hiatus. I'm pleased with the way *Walkout* turned out; it's a very, very powerful piece."

The closing moments of season two saw Admiral Adama reluctantly fleeing from a Cylon invasion force and also had his real-life alter ego donning a mustache at the request of the show's producers and director Michael Rymer, to illustrate the passing of a year. Edward James Olmos felt that the climax of 'Lay Down Your Burdens, Part II' marked an exciting end to a remarkable season of *Battlestar Galactica*.

"I think season two of *Battlestar Galactica* was the best season of television I've been involved with," he states. "It beat *Miami Vice* by a long shot. I felt season two was amazing. I never quite understood how the writers could get to that level. I was overwhelmed by the quality of the show in season two. The show seemed to consistently just get better and better and I thought the ending was just unprecedented.

"Season two really showed that *Battlestar Galactica* is the number one dramatic show in the world today," declares Olmos. "It actually left me anxious to get back to work for season three, and very excited about the future of the show." ∎

[LAURA ROSLIN]

"I will lead the people to salvation. It is my sole purpose."

No character gained more — or lost more — in *Battlestar Galactica*'s second season than Laura Roslin. Left behind bars and dying of terminal cancer at the end of the show's opening season, Roslin regained her Presidency and was cured of her cancer during season two, only to lose her role as the fleet's civilian leader in the season's closing moments.

"I felt season two was similar to season one in one way — Ron Moore, David Eick and the writing staff continued to take Laura into surprising territory," says Mary McDonnell of her character's arc in season two. "I was surprised by where she went and by many of the things she did, like ordering the assassination of Admiral Cain and the abortion of Sharon's baby. I really had to work with David and Ron at times to understand a lot of Laura's choices in the season and be able to show that she was making them cleanly, without ambivalence or sentiment.

"I think the big shift for Laura in season two is that the idea of taking the people to Earth, and their salvation, becomes her only focus," she notes. "There's no more ambivalence about it; she's learned to trust her instincts and she finds it easier to make quick decisions on the spot and live with the consequences of those decisions. Even after she is cured of cancer, reaching Earth remains her primary passion. Laura doesn't spend a lot of time talking or thinking about this major event she's been through or what it means. There's a little moment of euphoria and then she just goes back to work!"

Laura Roslin's rescue from terminal cancer in 'Epiphanies' represented a major development for the character, whose fight for life had previously been a key part of her arc. While McDonnell embraced the plot twist, she admits to having one reservation about the decision to end Laura's ongoing illness.

"The one thing that was difficult for me about Laura being cured was that I did feel I was abandoning the people out there with cancer," she explains. "We have a lot of fans who are struggling with cancer themselves, so I did experience a sense of guilt over the fact that Laura got this sudden cure-all that people in the real world can't have.

"But, overall, I thought Laura being cured was a great development for the show. I didn't want to play sick continually — that's tough to do on a television show, and it can be very limiting for the storytelling — and I thought the way Laura was saved raised some really interesting questions. I liked that she was saved by Cylon blood and that the person who saved her was Gaius Baltar — a man she's always felt cannot be trusted and later learns really is up to no good.

"Personally, I hope people think it's a good thing because it means Laura is still on the show," she adds with a smile. "During season one and the first half of season two, I had a lot of people say to me, 'Please don't tell me you're going to die.' A lot of people were worried Laura was going to be killed off, so I hope they are happy we haven't lost the character."

Season two of *Battlestar Galactica* developed Laura's antagonistic relationships with both Baltar and her other main political rival, Tom Zarek. The season also redefined Laura's interaction with another of her one-time adversaries, William Adama.

"Laura watches Adama change and experiences his openness in season two," McDonnell notes. "In the beginning, Adama had a lot of problems with Laura and he was an obstacle for what she was trying to do. But as the season develops, they become close allies and she gets a good chuckle out of Adama, because she can see how much he's softened. That can be a problem for her too, though, because Adama seems to become less willing to share the tough decisions with Laura."

As Laura built a new friendship with William Adama, she also found herself spending far less time with his son, Lee, and completely lost her two closest long-time allies: Billy Keikeya and Elosha. "The deaths of Billy and Elosha are very hard for Laura," says McDonnell. "She was used to facing her own mortality, but it was hard to deal with their deaths. The death of Billy in particular was shocking and deeply sad for Laura, because he represented the youth that was lost and the son she never had.

"Laura and Lee also went their different ways for season two, due to the nature of the storylines. That was disappointing for me personally, because I thought the friendship between those two very different characters was very interesting to explore."

The final hour of *Battlestar Galactica*'s second season sees Laura Roslin losing something else that was very dear to her — namely her position as the President of the Twelve Colonies of Kobol. McDonnell enjoyed exploring the drama inherent in Roslin's fall from power and subsequent return to her old life as a schoolteacher in 'Lay Down Your Burdens, Part II'.

"Losing the Presidency was very difficult for Laura," she notes. "It disengages her from the ability to try and ensure that civilization survives. While there's a part of her that enjoys teaching again, I don't think Laura really ever gives up on leading the people. She's an extremely committed woman."

Commitment is something Mary McDonnell shares with her *Battlestar Galactica* alter ego. By the end of her second season on the show, the two-time Academy Award nominated actress had absolutely no regrets about her decision to join the quest for Earth.

"This show has just been a huge blessing for me," she states. "I love the people I work with and I've been thrilled with the quality of the show. *Battlestar Galactica* is engaging the public in a way I find really gratifying — it's become very important to people — and that's very exciting to me." ■

[LEE ADAMA]

"I am not fit to wear the uniform. And maybe I never was."

Season two of *Battlestar Galactica* was truly a time of change for Lee 'Apollo' Adama. The season began with Captain Adama under arrest for mutiny and facing the possible end of his career, and concluded with Apollo as the Commander of his own Battlestar, the *Pegasus*. Along the way, Lee faced an existential crisis, nearly died (twice!) and confronted a dark secret from his past.

"Season two was great for my character," says Lee Adama's real-life alter ego, British actor Jamie Bamber. "Lee became much more independent and I actually enjoyed the second half of the season more than anything else I had done up to that point on the show. Lee had so much to do and was pushed to different extremes, and his journey was incredible.

"Lee gets pushed to rock bottom in season two," he notes. "Things get very dark for him around episodes ten, eleven and twelve ['Pegasus' and the 'Resurrection Ship' two-parter]. He finds everyone's behavior less than admirable during the war of wills between the *Galactica* and *Pegasus* crews. He starts to see humanity as being its own worst enemy and wonders if humanity really is worth saving. He reaches a nadir and tries to commit suicide. But he comes back from that and finds a new purpose through his assignment to the *Pegasus*. That was all great to play.

"The second half of season two also gives viewers an insight into Lee's past and why he behaves the way he does," Bamber continues. "'Black Market' reveals that he abandoned his lover when she told him she was pregnant and he's carrying a lot of guilt over that, especially because she was presumably killed in the Cylon attack on Caprica and he can't do anything to make it right. That was another very interesting development for my character. So I really didn't have a dull moment in season two!"

As well as revealing details of his lost love, *Battlestar Galactica*'s second season brought some new developments for Lee Adama's love life. After pursuing a relationship with the prostitute Shevon in 'Black Market', Lee shared a brief encounter with Kara 'Starbuck' Thrace before embarking on an ongoing romance with Anastasia Dualla.

"It was fun to explore Lee's passionate side," says Bamber, "and it was long overdue. It was a great way to find out more about Lee and how he ticks.

"I was happy that Lee ended up with Dualla," he reveals. "I don't know how long-term that relationship will be or how honest Lee is being about who he really wants to be with, but I think Lee and Dualla are a good match in many ways. Dualla is an oasis of calm and a strong presence who brings out the best in Lee. He's a more relaxed, peaceful kind of guy in her company.

"Lee sees in Dualla what he can never have in Starbuck. Lee and Kara are both screwed-up and self-loathing, and have commitment issues. And there are so many taboos about them getting together, because of Kara's relationship with Lee's brother, Kara and Lee's familial relationship with Admiral Adama and their officer-to-officer

relationship. So I think both of them realize it's really difficult for them to go there."

Away from Kara and Dualla, Lee's main relationship in season two is the one he shares with his father. "Lee's interaction with Adama was interesting to play in season two because it was much more solid than before," says Bamber. "They have slight differences, but they're more about specific issues rather than personal issues. They've grown to respect each other.

"Lee also comes to realize, albeit somewhat reluctantly, that he's a chip off his father's block. When's he promoted and becomes Commander of the *Pegasus*, I think he's surprised by how emotional he feels about the posting and ends up taking the reigns wholeheartedly. So there's a moment of realization that he has become his father after all.

"Of course, when Lee became the *Pegasus*' Commander, I did wonder how long it would last and whether it would even survive the rest of season two," Bamber admits with a laugh. "Being Commander of the *Pegasus* is a bit like marrying Starbuck — you know you could be in trouble!"

Despite Bamber's concerns, the end of season two revealed that Lee Adama was destined to survive at least a year as the Commander of the *Pegasus*. Yet while Bamber was pleased to learn of the *Pegasus*' survival, his initial reaction to the time-jump featured in 'Lay Down Your Burdens, Part II' was far less ecstatic. "The year jump left me cold at first," he reveals. "It smacked of gimmickry and I didn't understand why they were doing it. But when I learned that season three would fill the gaps, I changed my mind. I now think it was a worthy endeavor; it's clever and good television, and an exciting way to set up season three."

One of the many surprises contained in the closing moments of 'Lay Down Your Burdens, Part II' was the sight of a Lee Adama who had gained some thirty pounds during the settlement on New Caprica. "That was so much fun," says Bamber. "If you play the same character for eight months, it's a joy to go to work one day and get transformed. There was initially talk of me wearing a wig and the script referred to Lee having a beard, but when we tried those prosthetics on my face, we all thought it would be fantastic."

By the conclusion of *Battlestar Galactica*'s second season, viewers' perceptions of Lee Adama had certainly been tested and stretched by events in the season. In the process, Jamie Bamber believes the character became a more intriguing, believable and complex protagonist. "Season two took the shine off Lee in many different ways and I think that's made him a much more interesting character," he states. "We really see in season two that there are sides to Lee that aren't heroic. He can make bad decisions, he can piss people off and he can be uncommunicative and distant at times. But he's also, fundamentally, still a good guy. He tries to do the right thing and he has objectivity and a conscience that are his own. He remains a strong character who people are drawn to in dark moments." ■

[KARA THRACE]

"I'm fighting 'cause I don't know how to do anything else..."

The Colonial fleet's most famous Viper pilot found herself caught in a tailspin of pain, despair and self-destruction for the bulk of *Battlestar Galactica*'s second season — and Katee Sackhoff enjoyed every minute of it. "I thought season two was amazing for my character," says Sackhoff of her second season as Kara 'Starbuck' Thrace. "I felt Kara came into her own in season two; you really got to find out who she is and why she does things and what makes her tick. Episodes like 'The Farm' and 'Scar' revealed a lot about her and really made her face her demons.

"It was exhausting to play Kara's emotional turmoil, but it was a lot of fun for me too. It was also very rewarding; I feel I grew a lot as an actress during season two."

Season two begins with Kara on Caprica, where she encounters and enjoys a brief romance with Cylon-hating resistance fighter Samuel T. Anders (Michael Trucco). After reluctantly leaving Anders behind to return to the *Galactica*, Kara finds life on the Battlestar increasingly hard and hits the bottle, before realizing that she has fallen in love with Anders and needs to find a way to rescue him from Caprica.

"I had a fantastic through-line to play in season two," Sackhoff notes. "We saw Kara go to rock bottom and then find a new purpose in life, through Anders. She finally discovers she has something to fight for: Anders, a man she has fallen madly in love with and would give her life for.

"I loved that arc and I really liked what the introduction of Anders did for my character. I also enjoyed working with Michael Trucco, who's a great guy and a wonderful actor."

Kara's love for Anders not only changes her life but also complicates her relationship with Lee Adama. "Kara kind of finds herself in a love triangle with Anders and Lee," explains Sackhoff. "I loved the struggle between Lee and Anders — these two men who are so similar in many ways, yet so different in what they bring out of Kara. Anders is good for Kara, they're both strong yet vulnerable people who bring out the best in each other, whereas Kara knows she and Lee are not a good combination. Kara loves Lee, but she knows she brings out the worst in him.

"Kara's relationship with Lee seems to have deteriorated by the end of season two," she adds. "When we filmed the finale, Jamie Bamber and I didn't actually know what exactly had gone wrong between our characters. We played it as an extension of Lee being jealous of Kara and Anders, but everything was deliberately left open for season three."

As Kara finds herself increasingly estranged from Lee, she finds a new confidante in Karl 'Helo' Agathon. "Starbuck and Helo are old friends who have a very strong relationship," Sackhoff notes. "They can be very honest with each other because of that. I loved developing that relationship with Tahmoh in season two, especially because I hadn't worked with him since the miniseries."

Season two's two-part finale, 'Lay Down Your Burdens', completes Kara's arc by reuniting her with Anders. It then moves forward a year to show Kara living with Anders on New Caprica — as a married couple.

"I loved doing the finale and I thought the year-jump idea at the end was just an amazing thing to do," says Sackhoff. "I thought it was a clever twist and it allowed me to show a completely different side of Starbuck: she's married, she's settled down and she's probably at a point where she wants to have children. And, for the first time, we see her fighting to protect something — which is Anders and their future together.

"The finale also let me play Starbuck with longer hair, which is something I had to fight for," she continues. "I really had to persuade Ron and David to let me do that, because I wanted to show that Kara was showing her softer side. I thought that worked really well.

"What was funny about the finale was that when Michael Trucco heard Anders had married Starbuck, he said, 'That's it! I'm a dead man,'" she reveals with a laugh. "We all joked about how dangerous it was for him to marry Kara."

While the end of season two left Katee Sackhoff pondering Anders' fate and what exactly had happened during their year on New Caprica, one thing had become absolutely clear by the completion of shooting. Despite all the controversy that initially surrounded the *Battlestar Galactica* remake's transformation of Starbuck into a female Viper pilot, Sackhoff's character had succeeded in capturing the hearts and minds of viewers across the galaxy. "I think most people have really embraced our show and my character now," she states. "I think the show is really great and has become a big success, and I get an insane amount of fan mail these days. So I think we've definitely proven ourselves now and have shown just how extraordinary Ron Moore's vision for this series and these characters is." ■

"God has a plan for me."

Life for Dr Gaius Baltar took some startling turns during season two of *Battlestar Galactica*. The season not only marked Baltar's appointment as the President of the Twelve Colonies of Kobol, but also brought some major changes for James Callis' portrayal of the scientific genius and unwitting accomplice to the Cylons' near-annihilation of humankind.

"Baltar becomes a more miserable and more brutal character in season two," Callis explains. "Baltar has never been in a particularly happy place, but there were more laughs at his expense in season one and the miniseries. Even though his Presidential campaign starts out as a bit of a joke, Baltar himself is aware of that and he's generally far less of a comic foil in season two.

"Baltar's journey in season two really begins with the murder of Crashdown," he notes. "In some respects that was the right thing for Baltar to do, but it also feels like the worst thing he's ever done. That's Baltar's starting point for season two — and things don't get any better for him after that.

"I got to do a lot of really interesting things in season two and I enjoyed my character's arc," he says. "The idea of taking Baltar in a darker direction in season two really appealed to me, because I wanted Baltar to go on this journey in the hope of personal redemption — and constantly be unable to find it. Baltar isn't an out-and-out baddie or 'evil genius' type character. He's someone who wants to make up for the horrible things he is implicated in, but he's kind of cursed; he can't escape the past."

Naturally, Baltar's emergence as a darker and more dangerous character affected his relationships with everyone around him, especially the *Galactica*'s commander, William Adama, and Baltar's rival for the Presidency, Laura Roslin. "I think one of the main developments of the season for Baltar is that he reaches a point where he can tell Adama and Roslin to get lost," Callis notes. "Baltar would never have dared to have done that in season one or even at the start of season two, but after it becomes clear that Adama and Roslin have no faith in him and don't like him and think he's a Cylon agent, he feels he's had it with them."

Season two also maintained Baltar's relationship with Number Six by continuing his visions of Six and the ongoing mystery surrounding their origins. The season developed this dynamic by introducing another model of Number Six, Gina. "Baltar found something he thought was very special in Gina — a model of Number Six he could touch and hold," Callis explains. "Gina killing herself at the end of the season is a massive disaster for Baltar because of that. And it helps sell the idea that when Baltar takes over the Presidency, there are already ashes in his mouth."

Towards the end of season two, Callis received an opportunity to portray a very different version of Gaius Baltar. The episode 'Downloaded' features a Baltar who

haunts the first Number Six he encountered on Caprica in a series of visions. "That was a very interesting challenge," Callis recalls. "The Baltar who appears to Six is different from the one I normally play. It's complicated, but essentially I wanted to do things like find a voice for Baltar that a robot would have in its head.

"The interaction between Six and her Baltar is also very different from what we usually see between Baltar and the Six in his head. The Six in Baltar's head is constantly encouraging him to do bad things, but the Baltar in Six's head encourages her to do good things in 'Downloaded'."

Callis lists 'Downloaded' as one of his episodic highlights of *Battlestar Galactica*'s second season, alongside the pivotal death-of-Crashdown installment 'Fragged' and 'Resistance'. Another of Callis' most memorable season two episodes was 'Epiphanies'. "What I liked about 'Epiphanies' was that Baltar saves Roslin only because he actually wants to save the life of Sharon's baby and simply show how brilliant he is," Callis explains. "On some level, it's simply an act of narcissism. I thought that was a great idea."

Season two concludes on an electrifying note, with President Baltar facing the occupation of New Caprica. James Callis felt that the moving final scenes of 'Lay Down Your Burdens, Part II' provided an excellent end to *Battlestar Galactica*'s second season. "I thought the finale was great and I loved those closing moments on *Colonial One*," he states. "Before we shot them, David Eick said to me, 'Hef for Pres!' He wanted *Colonial One* under Baltar to be a bit like Hugh Hefner and the Playboy mansion. We also felt that Baltar, in that year on New Caprica, would have become increasingly Machiavellian and paranoid. We figured he'd have lots of people working for him and would become increasingly isolated — there are people he will meet and the non-supporters, who he won't meet. It was a really interesting way for us to end the season and it showed a different Baltar than we'd seen before." ■

[NUMBER SIX]

"If you have faith, everything will turn out exactly as it should."

Tricia Helfer stunned viewers in more ways than one during the second season of *Battlestar Galactica*. Season two not only saw the Canadian supermodel-turned-actress continuing to heat up the screen as the sexy and seductive Number Six that resides in Gaius Baltar's mind, but also allowed her to surprise viewers with two other incarnations of the Cylon siren.

"Season two was interesting for me, in several different ways," Helfer notes. "The arc for the Number Six in Baltar's head became driven by her concern for the Cylon-human baby and the idea that she wanted Baltar to protect it. She also pushed Baltar to become President and settle down on the planet in the latter half of the season. The main challenge of that arc for me was to play it in a way that seemed fresh and new. I tried to find different ways to portray Six's sensuality and physicality.

"The second half of the season was really exciting for me, because it allowed me to expand on Number Six by playing the Gina model and the original Number Six — the one we first saw in the miniseries," she continues. "I was particularly excited about playing Gina. She was so unlike any of the other Number Sixes we had seen before and I knew she was going to be a very challenging character to play."

Gina makes her first appearance in the pivotal second season installment 'Pegasus', when the humanoid Cylon is introduced as an abused prisoner of the Battlestar *Pegasus'* crew. After being freed from the *Pegasus* by Gaius Baltar, Gina finds shelter with the Cylon sympathizers before killing herself in the season finale, 'Lay Down Your Burdens, Part II'.

"Gina was the first Number Six we've seen that has been deeply traumatized," Helfer says of the character. "Unlike the other Number Sixes we'd seen up to that point, she wasn't in control and her psyche had been damaged. Through Gina, we discovered that humanoid Cylons can suffer pain and be emotional and vulnerable just like human beings.

"I researched a lot of things like post-traumatic stress syndrome to play Gina," she reveals. "When we first see her, I tried to make Gina a wounded animal — she lashes out to protect herself, just like a wounded animal would. After she escapes the *Pegasus*, she finds a safe haven [with the Cylon sympathizers] and puts all her energy into political activism, because she wants revenge for what was done to her and wants the humans to suffer. She ultimately gets that revenge by killing herself in a way that alerts the Cylons to the humans' plan to colonize New Caprica."

Gina's arrival also enabled the series to show a different kind of relationship between Baltar and a Number Six. "Gina and Baltar have a friendship and they rely on each other, but they don't have an intimate relationship until their very last meeting," Helfer explains. "It's only when Gina knows she has to kill herself to warn the Cylons that she gives herself to him. That's a very emotional scene between the two characters — it's not really sexy or crazy, it's more sad than anything else."

Helfer always knew that Gina was destined to die during the second season of *Battlestar Galactica* and initially thought the character would not survive the end of the multi-episode 'Pegasus' story arc. She was pleased that Gina actually lived on until the season's closing installment and feels it provided a fitting end to the character's emotional journey. "Viewers had a very strong response to Gina — they were really drawn to her — so I wanted her death to be a sad moment," Helfer recalls. "I really wanted it to tug at people's emotions. Gina is a Cylon, but when you know what was done to her, she becomes a much more sympathetic character. She's someone who has suffered enormously and what she really wants is to end her pain."

Before shooting Gina's demise in 'Lay Down Your Burdens, Part II', Helfer found herself playing a Number Six viewers had not seen since the first part of the *Battlestar Galactica* miniseries. The late second season installment 'Downloaded' cast Helfer as the Six who seduced Baltar to aid the Cylons' destruction of the Colonies and later gave her life to save him from a nuclear blast.

"The Six we see in 'Downloaded' is somewhere between Gina and the militaristic Caprica Six we saw in season one," Helfer notes. "She's suffered a trauma of her own and is struggling to deal with her feelings for Baltar, as well as having a Baltar in her head. That Six forms a bond with the 'Boomer' Sharon and together they convince the Cylon empire to rethink what they're doing. They point out that the Cylons are becoming what they detest and convince them to reconsider their course of action. I thought that was an interesting idea and it raised a lot of possibilities for season three."

Events in 'Downloaded' and 'Lay Down Your Burdens' left Tricia Helfer with many unanswered questions about the Cylons' master plan and the connection between Number Six and Baltar. They also left her keen to return to the *Battlestar Galactica* sets for the show's third year.

"The Cylons' master-plan was definitely still taking shape in season two," Helfer states. "I get the sense the writers have a general idea of where it's all going, but their ideas constantly change and evolve.

"There were times in season two when it was hard to play a character who seems to have all the answers, when you yourself don't know what those answers are, but that kept me on my toes and kept me excited about finding out where everything is going. I'm looking forward to finding out the answers to everything just as much as the audience." ∎

[SHARON VALERII]

"You said that humanity never asked itself why it deserved to survive. Maybe you don't..."

L ike the show's opening episodes, much of *Battlestar Galactica*'s second season required Grace Park to portray two models of Sharon Valerii, the humanoid Cylon otherwise known as Number Eight. But in a change from season one, her characters' arcs were totally reprogrammed for the show's sophomore year. While Park spent most of season one discovering her true Cylon nature as the undercover 'Boomer' Sharon, Park's primary role in season two was as the Number Eight originally known as 'Caprica Sharon' — and that Sharon's presence on the *Galactica* was a constant source of intrigue and mystery.

"Season two was fabulous for me," says Park. "I felt very fortunate to get the opportunity to play not one but two characters with major arcs. The things I got to do as the Sharon on *Galactica* were particularly exciting. A lot of it was horrible stuff in terms of content — abuse, assault, abortion, you name it — but all of those things were huge acting challenges that made me really push myself.

"I had a great time and I actually enjoyed myself in season two a lot more than I did in season one. I was extremely stressed during the making of season one — I put a lot of pressure on myself, just because I was so determined to do justice to the material — but this year I was a lot more confident and relaxed."

Caprica Sharon begins her stay aboard the *Galactica* early in season two, during the 'Home' two-parter. As the season progresses Sharon forges an uneasy alliance with William Adama, seemingly based on her desire to live and give birth to her half-human, half-Cylon baby. But throughout the season, Sharon's true motives and feelings for those around her — including her human lover, Lieutenant Karl 'Helo' Agathon — remain something of a mystery.

"There is a question throughout season two about whether what Sharon is doing is all a ploy," Park notes. "Sharon is a Cylon and has a Cylon point of view, so we don't know if she's really trying to help the humans or not. The way she's treated by the humans in season two, you could understand if she decided not to help them.

"The season also puts Sharon's relationship with Helo to the test," she continues. "By the end of the season, you are left wondering if Sharon and Helo are still together, and whether Sharon loved Helo just because they were having a baby together."

Season two's most memorable developments for Sharon included the birth of her baby in 'Downloaded'. While Park enjoyed shooting the pivotal episode, she readily admits that she initially disliked the idea of Sharon naming her baby Hera. "It seemed to suggest that Sharon named her baby after a human or Colonial god, which didn't make sense to me," she explains. "I really didn't like that idea at first. But I talked to Tahmoh about it, and we figured maybe she did it for Helo."

As Caprica Sharon embarked on a difficult new life aboard the *Galactica*, the

Battlestar's previous resident Number Eight, 'Boomer' Sharon, experienced death and resurrection. The death of Boomer was conceived by Ronald D. Moore as a way of surprising the audience and was welcomed by the character's real-life counterpart. "When I heard about the death of Boomer, I was actually quite pleased," Park recalls. "I remember thinking it was going to be a surprising and powerful moment for the audience, and I felt it was a great end to that part of the character's original arc. The character has been so tortured and conflicted and in such internal agony for so much of season one, I really felt killing her was a great way to end that part of her arc."

At the time of shooting 'Resistance', Park had no idea if Boomer would be seen again in the series. But some six months after the character's demise, Park found herself reprising her original role in the Cylon-centric episode 'Downloaded'.

"I initially had mixed feelings about returning to Boomer," Park reveals. "At first, I didn't want to bring her back. I'd spent so long as the other Sharon and I really liked her arc, and I felt we'd given Boomer a great arc and brought it to a terrific end. But there was also a part of me that missed playing her — Boomer was the character viewers originally connected to in the miniseries and season one — and I did miss the fun of playing two characters.

"Returning to Boomer was actually one of the biggest challenges of the season for me, because I had to work out where she'd been and what was going on in her head. When we see Boomer in 'Downloaded', she's changed in certain ways. She's realized she is a Cylon, but is still struggling with how she should deal with that. She's trying to hang on to her old human life at first, but at the same time she knows she can't go back to the *Galactica*. So that was an exciting development for that character."

The closing moments of season two's final episode, 'Lay Down Your Burdens, Part II', raise questions about Boomer's new relationship with her Cylon brethren. They also left viewers wondering about the fate of Caprica Sharon following Hera's birth and abduction.

"Ron Moore, David Eick and the writers wanted to leave things open for my characters at the end of the season," says Park. "I asked about it and I was told we'd find out what had happened to Sharon in the next season. When I heard that, I was like, 'Okay, when do we start shooting season three?' I'm very excited about finding out what's next for my characters." ■

[SUPPORTING CHARACTERS]

"Battlestar Galactica has exceptional supporting characters. You can throw pretty much anything at any of these characters and the actors can hold the center of the screen and really shine." — Michael Rymer

Michael Hogan feels that the second season of *Battlestar Galactica* truly fulfilled Ronald D. Moore's desire to explore the value and the flaws of the *Galactica*'s second-in-command, **Saul Tigh.** "I think Tigh developed incredibly in season two," Hogan explains. "He discovered his limits and realized why he never wanted to be a commander. He always knew he did not want a command of his own, but he came to understand exactly why.

"Tigh also realized that his life is with the military: he's a warrior, a career soldier, and that's what he does," he continues. "His lot in life is to protect people's ability to live their lives of freedom. Tigh becomes much more aware of that in season two and he accepts it. You can see that in the final episode ['Lay Down Your Burdens, Part II'], when Tigh is still trying to hang on to the military aspect of his life. He's an old soldier and he feels someone's got to stay and fight."

The other key element of Colonel Tigh's character arc for season two was its examination of Tigh's relationship with his commanding officer, William Adama. Season two revealed Tigh and Adama's long history and explored the depth of Tigh's feeling for "The Old Man".

"Adama is like a brother or a father to Tigh," Hogan notes. "He's the only family Tigh has got, apart from his wife Ellen. Tigh has lost many friends and associates over the years, but he's been through a lot with Adama. And in season two, I think they actually become closer friends."

While Tigh's bond with Adama went from strength to strength in season two, the Colonel's marriage remained an ongoing source of drama and tension. "Tigh's relationship with his wife is very challenging for him," says Hogan. "Tigh loves Ellen, but Ellen has a huge appetite for fun and life, and it doesn't take long for her to get bored aboard the *Galactica*. That creates a lot of trouble between them."

Tigh's continuing struggle with his wife, coupled with his ongoing battles with both the Cylons and alcoholism, meant that the character provided season two with plenty of

Above: (from left to right) Tigh, Lieutenant Felix Gaeta, Chief Galen Tyrol and Commander William Adama in 'Home, Part I'.

memorable dramatic moments. They also ensured that Michael Hogan continued to savor life aboard *Battlestar Galactica*.

"I had a blast on season two," he states. "Tigh is a fascinating character to play; he's a complex and believable character with a rich history. Season two was full of surprises and challenges for me, and I enjoyed them all."

Galen Tyrol was required to do far more than repair Vipers and Raptors during the second season of *Battlestar Galactica*. "Season two gave me much more challenging and thought-provoking stuff to do," explains the actor behind Tyrol, Aaron Douglas. "Tyrol wasn't just walking around Vipers doing the tech talk in season two; he had a lot of other things to do.

"At the start of the season, I was shooting the Cylons and being heroic," he notes. "That stuff was a lot of fun, but it was tough because people close to Tyrol kept dying — they started calling me 'The Angel of Death' on the set! After that, episodes like 'Resistance', 'Flight of the Phoenix' and 'Lay Down Your Burdens, Part I' were really big for Tyrol."

Much of Tyrol's arc for season two was driven by his feelings for his former lover, Sharon Valerii. As the season developed, Tyrol found his life turned upside down by the

Opposite: Tyrol in 'Resistance'.

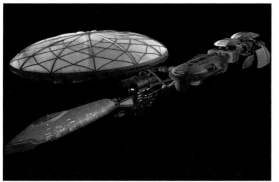

Cloud Nine Luxury Liner

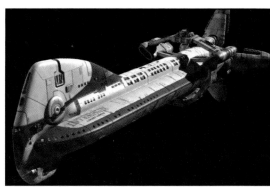

Colonial One Commercial Transport

Prison ship

Salvage and Repair Platform

Geminon Traveler Freighter/Transport

Luxury Liner (Intersun Passenger Cruiser)

Space Park Intersun Ring Liner

Cylon Base Star

The hotel room set from 'Black Market'.

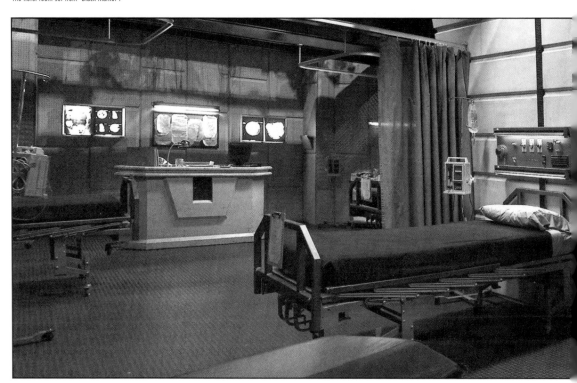

The sickbay set.

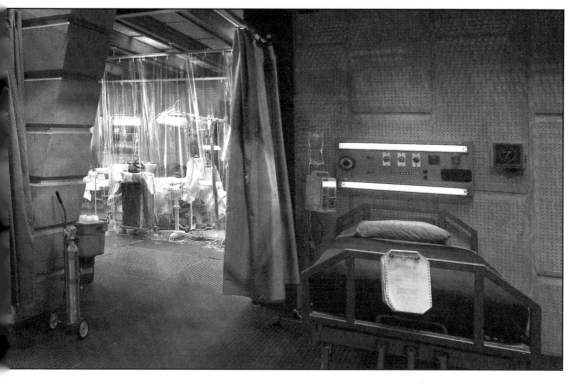

The *Galactica* faces a heavy Cylon assault in 'Scattered'.

Lieutenant Louanne 'Kat' Katraine finds herself in a tight spot during an asteroid target drills Viper pilot exercise in 'Home, Part I'.

'Boomer' Sharon's exposure as a Cylon, Boomer's death, and the subsequent arrival of a second Number Eight Cylon.

"At the start of season two, Tyrol is pulled out of his denial about Sharon being a Cylon and then has to face her death," Douglas explains. "He finds himself tormented by all that and questions whether he really ever could love Sharon. Tyrol's problems increase when Sharon and Helo turn up. He becomes really angry with Helo, although he's not sure why.

"But Tyrol's arc changes during the second half of the season. He realizes he needs to put it behind him and he needs to let this new Sharon be with Helo. I was glad about that, because it allowed me to explore some new territory."

Season two's finale, 'Lay Down Your Burdens', brought several surprising changes for Tyrol — including a new love interest, in the form of Cally. "I was shocked by that," Douglas admits. "At first, I did think to myself, 'I'm not sure I want to go there, guys…' I know some of the show's fans had predicted the characters were going to get together, but I'd always seen Tyrol and Cally as having a brother/sister relationship. Fortunately, I think the way they did it — with Tyrol being oblivious to it until Cally finally tells him — worked well."

The closing moments of the season two finale also required Douglas to grow a beard and wear glasses to play a Tyrol who had become New Caprica's union leader. "The beard and glasses were David Eick's idea," says Douglas. "He had seen me with a beard during the first season hiatus and he knows I wear glasses when I watch football games, and he had told me he had wanted to find a way of showing Tyrol in a beard and glasses."

After his character spent all of season one stranded on Caprica, Tahmoh Penikett was thrilled that *Battlestar Galactica*'s second season saw **Lieutenant Karl 'Helo' Agathon** rejoining his former crewmates aboard the *Galactica*. "It was great to be integrated into the core group for season two and get to work with the rest of the cast again," Penikett explains. "As much as I enjoyed working with Grace Park on season one, it was exciting to share some scenes with the other actors, especially Edward James Olmos and Mary McDonnell. And Helo's return to the *Galactica* opened a lot of doors for the character."

On returning to the *Galactica*, Helo immediately found himself at odds with his crewmates due to his ongoing relationship with his Cylon lover Sharon Valerii. Helo's struggle to overcome his crewmates' distrust and protect Sharon and their unborn child provided the basis of the character's arc for season two.

"The through-line for my character in season two concerns the love between this man and a Cylon, and the idea that they're going to have a child together," Penikett notes. "One of the things I found really interesting about that is the fact that Helo himself has conflicted feelings about it. He absolutely loves Sharon, but at the same time he's not oblivious to his crewmates' belief that he's betrayed them and the entire human race. So he has deeply conflicted feelings about Sharon and their child. I found that really intriguing to play."

Opposite: Lieutenant Karl Agathon in 'Resurrection Ship, Part I'.

Season two also developed Helo's friendship with Kara Thrace and saw him forge a unique bond with Chief Tyrol. "When Helo returns to the *Galactica*, the animosity and prejudice he faces is worse than he ever expected," Penikett says. "He finds there are only a few people who trust him, and Kara is one of them. Kara and Helo have been friends for a long time and have a buddy/buddy, brother/sister relationship; Helo is the only character Kara can confide in.

"Helo and Tyrol have an interesting relationship in season two," he continues. "I think everyone expected there to be some ongoing animosity between them over Sharon, but instead their love for Sharon actually brings them together. To their knowledge, they're the only humans who have fallen in love with Cylons — so they're the only people who can understand what the other is going through.

"I think we're all happy we went in that direction with the Helo/Tyrol relationship," he adds. "I know Aaron and I both felt a love triangle would have been too soap opera-ish."

While season two ends with Helo serving in the *Galactica*'s CIC, its closing moments left viewers pondering if Helo and Sharon's relationship had survived the apparent death of their child. "I know at one point we were going to see Helo and Sharon together after the year jump," Penikett reveals. "I believe there was going to be a scene where Helo and Sharon were in the *Galactica*'s canteen, and Helo was protecting her. But I think Ron Moore and David Eick decided they wanted to leave things open for next year and dropped it.

"I think that was a really intriguing thing to do," he notes. "It was a great way to keep people guessing!"

Kandyse McClure enjoyed developing **Anastasia Dualla** beyond her role as the *Galactica*'s principal communications officer during season two of *Battlestar Galactica*. "When we were doing season one, the running joke on-set was that I was the new Uhura," McClure reveals. "But season two really proved that wrong! Starting with her confrontation with Commander Adama in 'The Farm', I got a lot of exciting things to do.

"Dualla found herself in some surprising situations in season two," she notes. "She went from being a girl to being a woman in so many different ways. She also got her first name — Anastasia — which I think is a lovely name. It's very her."

Several of season two's biggest surprises for Dualla concerned her relationships with Billy Keikeya and Lee Adama. After establishing an ongoing attraction and flirtation between Dualla and Billy in the miniseries and first season, Ronald D. Moore decided to develop Lee into another suitor for Dualla and created a love triangle between the three characters.

"Dualla has to face that age-old conflict between choosing the nice guy or the bad boy," McClure explains. "Billy is the nice guy and Lee Adama is the bad boy. Dualla feels safe and comfortable with Billy, but it was a passionless and convenient coupling. Dualla's

Opposite: Anastasia Dualla in 'Sacrifice'.

relationship with Lee gives her a chance to be womanly and spend time with a very strong man.

"I enjoyed playing the intimate scenes between Dualla and Lee with Jamie Bamber," she adds. "I wanted to show a different side of Dualla in those scenes and show that she isn't self-conscious."

Season two concluded with Dualla and Lee Adama still together, serving aboard the Battlestar *Pegasus*. "The end of season two was a big surprise for all of us," McClure notes. "We found out Dualla had become a Lieutenant, although it's something of an empty promotion because she's mainly been promoted because there's no one else around. We also saw her with her hair down, which I was very pleased about."

"The finale left a lot of things open-ended," she notes. "It definitely was an intriguing way to end the season."

Felix Gaeta transformed himself from CIC officer to Presidential aide during *Battlestar Galactica*'s second season, in what Alessandro Juliani believes is an entirely logical development for his character. "I think Gaeta lost a lot of his illusions about military life during season two," Juliani notes. "He was something of an idealist in the miniseries and even season one, but in season two you can see that changing. 'Final Cut' and Gaeta's temper tantrum in 'Flight of the Phoenix' hint at his frustration with things and show that he's reflecting on what he wants to do with his life and where he fits in. 'Final Cut' also hints at the character's wild side; it suggests he's exploring new things socially that he might not have been exposed to before."

Gaeta's arc for season two culminated in the character being revealed as the aide to President Baltar. "That was an interesting twist for me — to discover that Gaeta had left the military to serve Baltar," Juliani recalls. "But it wasn't entirely unexpected as we'd laid the foundation for that in the miniseries and season one; we'd established Gaeta's admiration for Baltar."

In addition to finding a new role in life, Gaeta claimed a first name during season two — Felix. Juliani is quick to give the name his seal of approval. "I thought that was fantastic," he says. "It's a sufficiently tightly-wound name, yet it also suggests an underlying happiness — Felix is Latin for happy or fortunate."

Juliani's satisfaction with his character's first name extends to season two's overall treatment of Gaeta. "I think viewers learned quite a bit about Gaeta in season two and I got a lot of fun stuff to do," he states. "I really love where he ended up; I thought the finale was just outstanding."

Paul Campbell feels that **Billy Keikeya** did a lot of growing up during his second and final season of *Battlestar Galactica*. "Billy went from being the shy assistant to being much more of a self-thinking, independent man in season two," Campbell explains. "He found his voice and got to stand up to President Roslin a little more and started making his own political decisions. We also finally got to see more of the character's skills — we saw he

Opposite: Billy Keikeya in 'Sacrifice'.

was a genius in diplomacy and public relations and that kind of stuff."

Before his heroic demise in 'Sacrifice', Billy also continued his will they/won't they relationship with Anastasia Dualla during season two. Billy's pursuit of Dualla was complicated by Lee Adama's emergence as a rival for her affections. "I thought the Billy/Dualla story took some interesting turns in season two," Campbell notes. "It would have been exciting to see where it all would have gone if I'd stayed on the show."

Following his decision to leave the show, Campbell feels proud to have played such a popular supporting role on *Battlestar Galactica*. "I loved every single second of my time on *Galactica* — even days when I didn't have any lines," he states. "I wouldn't trade a single second of it for anything. It was so much fun and I learned a lot. Working with Mary McDonnell and Eddie Olmos was a bit like being paid to take acting classes from some of the greats in the industry.

"I do miss being a part of *Galactica*," he admits. "I feel its loss. It's hard to know you chose to leave a great show."

From killing the 'Boomer' Number Eight to finding love with Galen Tyrol, **Cally** surprised viewers more than once during *Battlestar Galactica*'s second season. "Season two was amazing for my character," says Cally's real-life alter ego, Nicki Clyne. "I got a lot of challenging and interesting scenes to work on and I was very grateful to be a part of some important storylines.

"Cally's arc for the season really begins with her experiences on Kobol," Clyne notes. "Her time on Kobol leaves her traumatized, and also brings her closer to Tyrol. That leads to her killing Boomer — whom she blames for Tyrol being locked up and accused of being a Cylon — and then later telling the Chief how she feels about him. I thought her arc made complete sense, because of everything that happened on Kobol."

Cally's arc for season two concluded with the character at Tyrol's side — and heavily pregnant! "When I first read the script for the finale ['Lay Down Your Burdens'], I was amazed to see my character going from being beaten up to being pregnant and apparently leading the normal life she had wanted since the start of the series," Clyne reveals. "That was definitely an interesting place to go!

"What was funny about it was that when I went on set to shoot Cally's last scenes, a lot of the crew didn't recognize me," she adds with a laugh. "When they saw me in a dress and with the 'pregnant belly', people just couldn't believe it was me!"

He may be the only star of the original series to crossover into its modern remake, but Richard Hatch certainly doesn't take his place in the new *Battlestar Galactica* for granted. "I honestly thought **Tom Zarek** was going to end up being killed in season two," he reveals. "I thought the way Tom seemed to be scheming with Meier in 'Home', he was going to end up dead with him."

Fortunately, Hatch's concerns about Zarek proved to be ill-founded. The character

Opposite: Tom Zarek, and Number Six, in 'Lay Down Your Burdens, Part II'.

survived season two's civil war story arc and went on to play a key role in the Presidential election campaign, as none other than Gaius Baltar's running mate.

"The big change for Zarek in season two is that he really tries to find a way to operate within the system," Hatch says of his character's development. "In season two, Zarek tries to forward his agenda within the traditional boundaries of the system, rather than with violence. You can see that in his political alliance with Baltar and also his dealings with President Roslin, when he helps her oppose a military dictatorship and restore the civilian government.

"I still think Zarek is driven by a desire to do good," he adds, "but at the same time he's also been damaged by the past and has become very distrustful of politicians and people in positions of authority. That makes him feel he has to play the game better than them: he has to be even more adept than they are at all the manipulation, intrigue and coerciveness. It was fascinating to explore that in season two."

Zarek's continued pursuit of political power took many twists and turns during season two, in a manner which stunned Hatch just as much as the show's audience. "Ron Moore always seems to find the most interesting and most surprising ways to develop the story and characters," he states. "I thought the show became richer, deeper and more profound in season two. I also thought the show weaved more elements of the original series into its fabric for season two, like the mythology and the sense of camaraderie and family between the characters. That was a smart move."

"My character went from a rookie pilot to *Galactica*'s top gun," says Luciana Carro of her role as **Lieutenant Louanne 'Kat' Katraine** in *Battlestar Galactica*'s second season. "I was so thrilled by what they gave me to do. I loved my character's arc for season two.

"At the start of the season, we find out that Kat has been using stims to stay awake and keep her edge, and she's actually become addicted to them — she almost kills herself when she crashes her Viper in 'Final Cut'. But she goes through detox after that and comes back more determined than ever, which leads to her replacing Starbuck as the *Galactica*'s top gun."

A young Canadian actress whose screen credits include recurring roles in the shows *Everwood* and *Da Vinci's Inquest*, Carro made her début as Kat in *Battlestar Galactica*'s first season episode 'Act of Contrition'. She was cast as Kat after auditioning for the show's makers.

"I really wanted to be a part of *Battlestar Galactica* because I loved the original series — I watched it as a kid — and the new show is just so fantastic," she recalls. "I also liked the sound of my character: she was described as someone who was feisty and determined and had a lot of attitude; she's someone who likes to test authority.

"When I read for the role, I went into the audition with my Xbox joystick and used that as my Viper control pad," she reveals with a laugh. "I guess that must have helped me stand out from the others!"

Donnelly Rhodes believes that season two's treatment of **Doctor Cottle** is worthy of a clean bill of health. "Cottle was around a bit more in season two than he was in season one, and I think the show has worked out the best ways to make use of him," Rhodes explains. "The doctor seems to have established himself as an opinionated, crusty, benign character who relates to the other characters in interesting ways. For me, personally, he's become a symbol of the doctor's credo — do no harm. Sometimes he's forced to do things by Adama or Roslin that he doesn't agree with, but when that happens he'll always make his statement about it.

"Season two also seemed to develop the character's potential for humor, especially in episodes like 'Home, Part II'," he adds. "You get to see more of Cottle's wry sense of humor in season two."

Cottle saved numerous lives during season two, including those of William Adama and Laura Roslin. The season also saw him becoming involved in the intrigue surrounding Sharon Valerii's half-human, half-Cylon baby.

"I really enjoyed playing Doctor Cottle in season two," states Rhodes. "I got lots of interesting things to do and I've been flattered by people's response to my work. People seem to really like the character. I'm not entirely sure what I'm doing that people like so much, but I'm certainly not going to complain about it!"

The closing moments of *Battlestar Galactica*'s season two finale, 'Lay Down Your Burdens, Part II', featured the surprise return of Callum Keith Rennie as **Leoben**. "It was fun to come back for the finale," says Rennie, who previously played the humanoid Cylon in the second part of the *Battlestar Galactica* miniseries and the season-one episode 'Flesh and Bone'. "I was only in one scene, but I'm sure Leoben's return brought up a lot of questions about why he's there and what he's doing. The plan was for that to lead into me doing more on the show in season three."

Leoben was the first humanoid Cylon to be discovered by the crew of the *Galactica*. Following his initial encounters with William Adama and Kara Thrace, Leoben has become primarily known for his apparent ability to toy with and confuse his adversaries.

"I look at Leoben as a messenger," Rennie reveals. "He's someone who's always bringing information in one way or another — although the humans can't always be sure if that information is true. The thing I really like about Leoben is that he's not evil. He's perceived as a villain by the *Galactica*'s crew, but he's not villainous — he just has different ideas and values."

A prolific British-born, Canadian-raised actor, Rennie was originally offered the role of Leoben based on his earlier work in such diverse productions as *Due South*, *eXistenZ* and *Blade: Trinity*. "I didn't need much persuading to do *Battlestar Galactica*," he recalls. "I had watched the original series when I was young and I liked the idea of the new show — it was very character driven. I also liked the fact that all my scenes were with Edward James Olmos, who I knew would be fantastic to work with. So I agreed to do it and have enjoyed being a part of *Battlestar Galactica* ever since." ■

[PRODUCTION DESIGN]

> "The second season of a series gives you an opportunity to build on what you've done and fine-tune things, and maybe have a little fun with it too." — Richard Hudolin

Fresh from successfully creating a 'retro-futuristic' environment that combined familiar and unworldly elements to brilliant effect, the makers of *Battlestar Galactica* set out to expand the show's extraordinary visual universe with its second season. "We really wanted to develop our ideas during season two, while staying true to the basic look and feel we established in the miniseries and the first season," explains the series' production designer, Richard Hudolin. "You always learn a lot in the first year of a series, so we wanted to build on everything we'd accomplished in season one and just continue to deliver interesting design work."

"The writing on season two was very strong and clever, and it presented us with a lot of interesting design challenges," adds art director Doug McLean. "It was a great season for us to work on."

The biggest design challenge presented by *Battlestar Galactica*'s second season was undoubtedly the realization of the Battlestar *Pegasus*. First seen in the season's tenth installment, *Galactica*'s long-lost sister ship was destined to become a regular fixture of the show, as well as one of its most visually interesting shooting locations.

"Designing the *Pegasus* was a huge job," Hudolin reveals. "Going in, we knew the *Pegasus* was supposed to be a top-of-the-line ship, so we wanted to give it a new look that really evolved the design of the Battlestars. Our basic premise was the *Pegasus* was essentially the *Galactica* forty years more advanced. So while the *Galactica*'s design reflected the 1940s, the look of the *Pegasus* was rooted in the 1980s. I gave the ship a cold, corporate look and a different texture from the *Galactica* — there's a lot of glass and chrome and that sort of thing. I also wanted there to be less people in the control room, to reflect the idea the ship is more automated, and gave it a stylized dradis that comes down. And we used the ship's corridors to give a sense of the ship's scale."

Opposite: Concept artwork for Kara Thrace's apartment on Caprica and the "cramped and overcrowded rust-bucket freighter" seen in 'Scattered'.

With much of Stages G, H and I of Vancouver Film Studios already housing various permanent and temporary *Battlestar Galactica* sets, the construction of the *Pegasus* required the show to lease a fourth stage. The producers managed to secure Stage D, which ultimately influenced the ship's look. "Stage D is smaller and lower than the *Galactica* stage," explains Hudolin. "It was a tough design challenge, because the stage seemed too small for what we wanted to do and we were up against time, as we had to get the *Pegasus* done before

STAGE BY STAGE

Production of *Battlestar Galactica*'s second season was based on four stages of Canada's Vancouver Film Studios. Stage G housed the *Galactica*'s hangar bay and a green screen area that also played host to *Colonial One* when that set was required. The CIC and various temporary sets were based in Stage H, while Stage I housed the bulk of the *Galactica*, including the Battlestar's hallways and multi-purpose rooms. Stage D was leased early in season two to play host to the *Pegasus* sets.

BATTLESTAR GALACTICA 2

MICHAEL RYMER
RICHARD HUDOLIN
KEN RABEHL

DATE Mar 15/05 B2
Waterfall Building

Int. Kara's Apartment
Concept Illustration

42-3

BATTLESTAR GALACTICA 2

MICHAEL RYMER
RICHARD HUDOLIN
KEN RABEHL

MAR 15/05 B1

INT. SPACE FREIGHTER CREW QUARTERS
CONCEPT ILLUSTRATION

38-3

the mid-season break. We were really designing on the fly. But I think it came out well in the end. We were all pretty happy with the way it looked."

As the *Pegasus'* interior design took shape, Hudolin enlisted the show's visual effects department to develop the look of the Battlestar's exterior. The initial design work was performed by visual effects CG supervisor Doug Drexler, in collaboration with Hudolin and visual effects supervisor Gary Hutzel.

"We had to do a lot of passes at the exterior design of the *Pegasus*," Hutzel reveals. "There was initially some talk of us doing something that was completely different from the *Galactica*. There was concern that the viewers might get confused between the *Pegasus* and the *Galactica* if the ships were too similar. But after we did the first few designs, Ron Moore stepped in and made it clear that the *Pegasus* needed to be much more like the *Galactica* and just needed to look like a newer version of the *Galactica*.

"After that, we went out to the set to see the design work Richard and his team had done. We saw the ship's modern office look, with its regular panel patterns, and tried to put that on the exterior design. Eventually we went with the panel idea, with a lot of lighting. That was the departure point for us — the *Pegasus* has a lot more lighting than the *Galactica*, and that keeps the ships separate. Everyone was happy with that."

Another of season two's key spaceship designs was the Cylon Heavy Raider. Like the exterior of the *Pegasus*, this design was also developed by Drexler.

"I asked Doug to redesign the Heavy Raider at the start of season two because our early design was a little too wimpy, too smooth and just too unthreatening," Hutzel recalls. "We had been looking at the Heavy Raider as a land tank with rockets, but the initial designs were very squat and angular. Doug took a look at it and got rid of all its hard edges, so people would know it was a Cylon vessel. He also elongated it to make it sharp on the front and back, and gave it dual gatling guns as well as a lot of texturing.

"By the time he finished it, Doug got really excited about the design and put a four-foot by eight-foot print of the Heavy Raider on the wall of David Eick's office," continues Hutzel with a grin. "David came in and took one look at it and said, 'That's really cool. We need to feature that in the show!' And that's how it ended up in the season premiere, 'Scattered'."

As the Cylon Heavy Raider started to make its presence felt, Hudolin and his team concentrated on the creation of Chief Tyrol's home-made stealth fighter, the Blackbird. First seen in 'Flight of the Phoenix', the Blackbird was constructed with a poly-resin material that gave the ship a stealth-looking surface.

"Designing the Blackbird was a lot of fun," says Hudolin. "I remember telling Doug and

IIIII LOST IN TRANSLATION

During the development of the *Pegasus*, it was suggested that the production could rework elements of the sets from the unscreened 2004 John Woo pilot *The Robinsons: Lost in Space* to create the top-of-the-line Battlestar. But it soon became clear this wouldn't suit the design aesthetic of the show. "It was a good money-saving idea on the part of the producers," Hudolin notes, "but it wasn't going to work for us, because the *Lost in Space* sets were just so different from what we wanted to do. So in the end I said, 'Forget it! Let's do what we think is right and just go with it.' I think the only thing we ultimately used from the *Lost in Space* sets was a bit of a hallway!"

THE PRODUCER'S CUT

With Ronald D. Moore and David Eick dividing their time between the show's Los Angeles production office and its Vancouver sets, the day-to-day process of shooting *Battlestar Galactica*'s second season was supervised by the series' Vancouver-based producer, Harvey Frand. "I think season two was very strong," says Frand, who also served as the producer of the *Battlestar Galactica* miniseries and its first season. "Our goal for season two was to maintain the quality of the show, as well as everyone's interest in working on it. It was a bit of a marathon compared to the miniseries and the first season; season two was twenty episodes instead of thirteen episodes or a four-hour miniseries. But I feel really good about the way it came out.

"I'm really proud of season two," he continues, "and I think that's all down to our extraordinary cast and crew, our writing staff and, of course, Ron Moore. Ron is an extraordinary writer. I don't think I've ever worked with a writer who can adapt to financial and practical realities as well as Ron. If Ron or any of the other writers write something we can't afford to do, he can always come up with another way of finding the emotional content the show is looking for."

A veteran TV producer whose many credits include the series *Beauty and the Beast*, *Strange World* and *Young Riders*, Frand has no doubt that *Battlestar Galactica* represents a special project in his long and varied career. "I'd say this show is probably the highlight of my career," he states. "It's funny — Eddie Olmos and I are roughly the same age and we've both been in the business a long time, and we've discussed how lucky we are at this point in our careers to be a part of something that's as satisfying and good as this show. *Battlestar Galactica* is a really great series, and working on it has probably been the best experience I've had on a show."

Ken Rabehl, our assistant art director, that they had to treat it like a hot rod that had been built by someone in their backyard. They had to put it together like people who watch DIY shows. It became a really nice piece to work on because everyone who worked on it brought their own little touches to it."

In addition to designing ongoing shooting locales like the *Pegasus* sets, Hudolin and his team continued to produce various other sets for short-term use. These creations ranged from what Hudolin describes as "the cramped and overcrowded rust-bucket freighter" Adama and Tigh are seen serving on in 'Scattered' to Shevon's quarters in 'Black Market' and the distinctively different bars featured in 'Scattered', 'Black Market' and 'Sacrifice'. During the latter part of season two, the design team also constructed a new, full-sized Viper cockpit interior. This was initially for use in the episode 'Scar'.

"Each of our Vipers had a working cockpit within the fuselage, but they were proving difficult to film in," McLean explains. "So we built a much more functional cockpit as a separate unit. We tried to keep the look we'd previously established, but we made the cockpit more realistic and practical.

"The exciting thing about it is that the cockpit is largely aluminum, because it's largely built from practical elements. We actually salvaged a lot of the cockpit's parts from an aircraft graveyard."

Away from *Battlestar Galactica*'s soundstages, Hudolin also once again played a key role in seeking out shooting locations for the series. "We used a variety of locations in season two," he notes. "We seemed to be less city-bound. We went out to places like Maple Ridge, where we found an abandoned technical school that used to be a prison and turned it into the resistance headquarters. We also went back to Widgeon Slough for the Kobol sequences at the start of

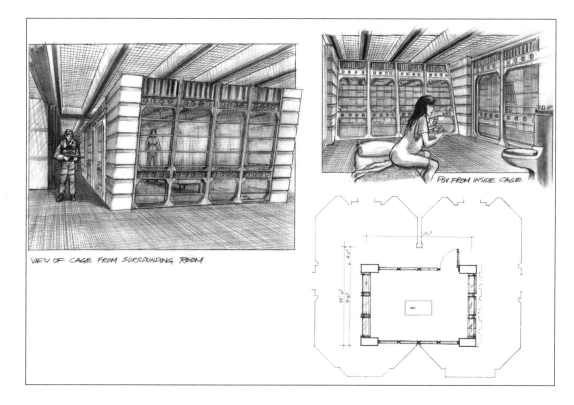

VIEW OF CAGE FROM SURROUNDING ROOM.

POV FROM INSIDE CAGE.

the season. Those scenes were challenging to shoot because we'd shot 'Kobol's Last Gleaming' the previous September and when we went back there for season two, it was April and the weather was completely different, but we still had to make everything match up.

"I think the most exciting location work we did was New Caprica," Hudolin adds. "We basically built a whole 'tent city' out in Richmond, and I think it looks great on screen."

Reviewing their department's contributions to *Battlestar Galactica*'s second season, Richard Hudolin and Doug McLean are understandably proud of the variety of memorable designs they managed to deliver. In fact, their only disappointment concerns what they didn't get to do. "We didn't get as heavily into the Cylon world in season two as I would have liked," McLean admits. "We had hoped to get inside a Cylon Heavy Raider in the season finale, but that disappeared because of costs. But everything else was just great."

"Overall, I think season two was another great year on the show for us," declares Hudolin. "You always wish you had more time and money, but it's just fantastic to be a part of this show." ∎

Above: Concept artwork for Sharon Valerii's prison-cell home on the *Galactica*.

[COSTUME DESIGN]

"We had to come up with a lot of different looks and costumes for season two. It was a season full of challenges." — Glenne Campbell

The second season of *Battlestar Galactica* provided the series' costume design department with an opportunity to open the Colonial wardrobe and really expand the show's clothes range. "There was a lot more costuming work to perform in season two than there was in season one," explains costume designer Glenne Campbell. "There was more variety in the clothing of the characters and the extras, pertaining to both the military and civilian aspects of the show.

"We've kept the '*Gilligan's Island* in space' idea: the main characters still don't have a lot of clothing to change into," she adds. "But the introduction of new characters and the change in the main characters' circumstances at the end of the season presented us with a lot of new challenges."

One of the biggest and most time-consuming costuming challenges concerned the creation of uniforms for the crew of the Battlestar *Pegasus*. While the uniforms were clearly rooted in existing Colonial military dress code, the task proved surprisingly complicated.

"We kept the basic look of the *Galactica* uniforms for the *Pegasus* crew, because the idea is that this is one military organization so the costumes would have come from the same supply system," Campbell notes. "But we wanted the *Pegasus* uniforms to have a crisper look and just be a cut above the *Galactica* uniforms, to show that the *Pegasus* is a top-of-the-line ship. We also changed the patch, to make it clear that the *Pegasus* crew were on a different ship from *Galactica*.

"We actually tried to match the fabric of the uniforms from the miniseries for the *Pegasus* outfits," she continues, "but the supplier didn't have any more of the fabric and we learned that the mill in Europe that made the fabric had closed. So we then had to find a way of duplicating the fabric. We finally found a mill in Vancouver that wove the fabric for us in black

Below: Lucy Lawless asked *Battlestar Galactica*'s costume-designers to give D'Anna Biers' clothing a distinctive look.

and we then sent the fabric to another company which dyed it in the Air Force blue and black look! It was a tremendous challenge to get all that done in time."

Season two also required Campbell and her team to dress the various members of the Caprica resistance, including the new love of Kara Thrace's life, Samuel T. Anders. "We wanted to give those costumes a hint of contemporary relevance as well as a futuristic feeling," Campbell recalls. "We gave them layers of clothing to suggest they could survive in the mountainous terrain they were in, and we gave the costumes an earthly feeling to suggest they could hide in the earth if they needed to."

The introduction of the Caprica resistance was followed a few episodes later by the arrival of Lucy Lawless as D'Anna Biers in 'Final Cut'. Dressing D'Anna provided *Battlestar Galactica*'s costume department with another opportunity to break new ground.

"Lucy came in and said to us, 'What can I do to look different from the other characters?'" Campbell explains. "I told her, 'That's really easy, because except for Ellen Tigh no one has any real adornment or accessories; most people are in uniforms.' So we gave her groomed fingernails and jewelry, and a big range of clothes. She was a fun character to dress."

Above: 'Lay Down Your Burdens, Part II' required new costumes for many of the show's main characters, including Kara Thrace.

A similar highlight of season two for Campbell and her colleagues concerned designing costumes for the later installment 'Black Market'. "That was an exciting episode for us," she notes. "We had to come up with a lot of costumes for that, and we wanted the costumes of the characters involved in the black market to have a hot, seductive feeling, to show how seductive consumerism is."

After successfully clothing all the new characters encountered by the *Galactica* and maintaining the wardrobes of the show's regular and recurring characters, Campbell and her team found themselves faced with one final challenge right at the end of season two. The season's closing installment, 'Lay Down Your Burdens, Part II', required the bulk of the show's main characters to don new costumes.

"The last episode was a huge amount of work for us," Campbell recalls. "We had to come up with new wardrobe for pretty much everyone, except for Adama. And we had to create a whole new look in a couple of weeks! But I think it came out great and it certainly was an exciting way to end the season." ∎

[VISUAL EFFECTS]

"We really wanted to develop our ideas in season two, in a way that always served the show's storylines." — Gary Hutzel

From the *Galactica* finding itself all alone in space to the Cylon Centurions' arrival on New Caprica, *Battlestar Galactica*'s second season was packed with memorable visual effects sequences. The creation of these computer-generated images was driven by the show's visual effects supervisor, Gary Hutzel, who saw season two as an opportunity to break further new ground for small-screen science fiction.

"My focus on *Galactica* has always been on serving the story and making the effects work within the context of the show," says Hutzel. "But with season two, I also hoped to generally advance the effects and introduce some new concepts by developing our in-house visual effects capability.

"I really wanted to start taking advantage of the producers' willingness to incorporate our ideas into the show in season two. The producers and directors are totally approachable to my ideas, just as I am open to theirs. Our show is unique in that if I want to introduce a new concept I can suggest it to Ron Moore and David Eick at the pre-production level. If they like it, they will actually change the script to suit it. So I wanted to develop our in-house visual effects capability, which would give us greater ability to explore our ideas while we continued to work with our usual external effects houses."

Hutzel began building *Battlestar Galactica*'s in-house effects staff at the start of season two, when he formed a CGI-rendering facility above Stage D of Vancouver Film Studios. The in-house facility's first staff members included veteran designer and effects artist Doug Drexler, whose many credits include *Star Trek: Enterprise*, *Star Trek: Deep Space Nine*, *Star Trek: First Contact* and the CG-animated series *Roughnecks: The Starship Troopers Chronicles*.

"I brought Doug Drexler in as the in-house CG supervisor to head the facility and develop some of the ideas I wanted to pursue," Hutzel recalls. "Doug's a great artist

Below: The Cylon Heavy Raider played a key role in the season-two premiere, 'Scattered'.

Above: The look of the CGI Cylon Centurions was developed extensively during season two.

and concept man, and I snapped him up as soon as *Enterprise* finished. We also brought on people like Adam 'Mojo' Lebowitz, who's another very talented effects veteran.

"'Scar' was a turning point for us because it was our first in-house show," he continues, referring to season two's fifteenth episode. "By doing it in-house we were able to do many shots that we otherwise wouldn't have been able to get. There are, I believe, sixty-five visual effects shots in that show and sixty-one of them were done in-house. The other four shots were finished by Atmosphere, because we couldn't quite get the flying blood to work in time.

"But my goal was never to do everything in-house," Hutzel adds firmly. "I just wanted to be able to put a lot more in the show, while still involving outside facilities to do certain things."

With the show's in-house visual effects artists in place, Hutzel divided season two's effects work between his staff and the series' primary external effects suppliers, the Los Angeles-based Zoic and the Vancouver-based Atmosphere. "We did quite a lot of shots in-house, but I think Atmosphere probably did the most number of shots for season two while Zoic did the most complex shots," Hutzel reveals. "I generally sent the most complex shots to Zoic, like the fussy 3D combined with 2D compositing type shots, because it has a big staff and can assign more people to meet tight deadlines. I also don't think anyone can do explosions quite like Zoic — their work on the destruction of *Cloud Nine* in 'Lay Down Your Burdens, Part II', for example, was just fantastic. But Atmosphere does terrific stuff too; they generally did all our matte paintings and set extensions on season two."

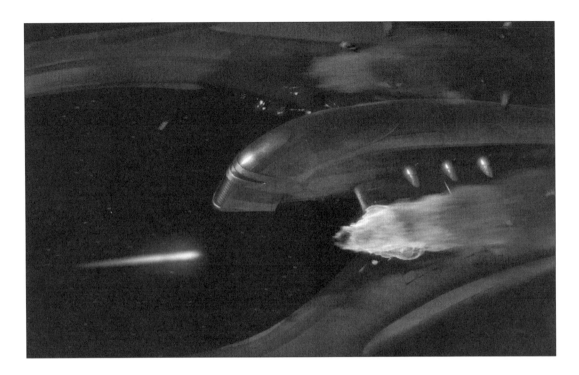

Above: Season two boasted some of *Battlestar Galactica's* most memorable visual-effect sequences to date.

Atmosphere also became primarily responsible for the show's Cylon Centurions, starting with season two's third installment, 'Fragged'. The episode saw the series employing cutting-edge high-definition imaging (HDI) for the first time to create unprecedentedly realistic Centurions.

"I wanted the show to use the latest technologies for render on the Cylons and Atmosphere agreed to invest the development time and man hours to do HDI," Hutzel explains. "It's a difficult process which involves reflection maps and creating the light effects on the Centurions from high resolution, but Atmosphere said they were a forward-thinking company and wanted to do it, and they got it done for the third episode.

"What we ended up with were much more realistic Centurions than we had had in the past. That was apparent in later episodes. The Centurions started to look like actual objects in the scene, as opposed to animated characters that had been added after shooting."

Season two also enhanced the movement of the Cylon Centurions from its third episode. "We made the Centurions' movement more anthropomorphic and have given them more human-like motion," Hutzel notes. "I think from a visual effects standpoint that was another turning point."

On a far more subtle note, season two also featured several new shots of the *Galactica* that showed the Battlestar from different angles. "We're not into stock shots on this show," Hutzel points out. "We're always trying to find new shots of *Galactica*, when it's appropriate to the show and the story.

"We had a bit of a problem on that in season two, because David Eick still wouldn't let us go underneath the *Galactica*. He wasn't sure people would know where they were on the *Galactica* if we did that. There's lots of cool stuff you can see from underneath — there's a docking port and all kinds of engines and structure and illuminated areas — but we weren't able to show it in season two."

Like season one and the miniseries before it, *Battlestar Galactica*'s second season employed a variety of software packages to produce its visual effects. These included LightWave, Digital Fusion and Combustion, which have been employed to create everything from epic space battles to the drops of blood seen in 'Resistance'. Season two has also continued *Battlestar Galactica*'s flexible approach to the creation and rendering of the show's effects, with sequences being reworked right through to the final editing process.

"Our episodes are really developed in post-production," explains Hutzel. "They're written and they're shot, but they're often completely reworked in post. The order of scenes and the ways scenes play out are often changed in post, and that obviously leads to changes to the effects sequences. I've had to work with the editors to re-cut entire visual effects scenes in post-production.

"It can be a lot of work, and it's crazy at times that we change stuff while we're racing to meet our deadlines, but I think it's been a good thing for the show. It's allowed us to be really creative and collaborative, and it's a long way from the old system in television effects where the effects crew would meet with the producers at the beginning, decide what the effects shots would be and then simply add them to the show in post-production. I think what we're doing represents the future of effects — there has to be more interactivity — and I'm glad we've continued to take this approach."

Gary Hutzel has no doubt that *Battlestar Galactica*'s flexible and collaborative approach to the visual effects process has played a crucial role in the series' success. He's also extremely pleased with everything he and the show's visual effects crew have achieved with season two. "Season two was very successful from the effects standpoint because we managed to tell all the stories Ron Moore wanted to tell," he states. "That doesn't always happen on a TV show; things often can't be done because of time or money or other factors. But we've managed to tell the stories Ron wanted to tell and we've kept the effects stylish and in budget. I'm very pleased about that." ■

SHOOTING TO THRILL

Since *Battlestar Galactica*'s launch as an episodic series, director of photography Stephen McNutt has played a key role in developing the unique visual style of the show. "I always try to give the show what we describe as a 'snotty' look," says McNutt, whose previous credits include *seaQuest DSV, The Dead Zone, American Gothic* and *The Cosby Mysteries*. "I've generally gone for an industrial feeling, with very industrial-type lighting, and have aimed to give viewers the sense they're in a flying warehouse. I also tend to use lighting to illustrate the vulnerability of the characters, because *Battlestar Galactica* is a show about vulnerability.

"I lit and shot season one with as much grit and intensity as I possibly could," he notes, "so the challenge of season two was to maintain and develop that. We wanted to maintain our edge and energy in season two, and I think we did that; I think season two represents a maturing of what we did in season one."

[MUSIC]

> "*Battlestar Galactica's* second season required a constantly-developing musical soundtrack. As the story arcs continued to expand and develop, the music also had to evolve." — Bear McCreary

Just like the series' characters and storylines, the music of *Battlestar Galactica* consistently developed in surprising and powerful ways during season two. After establishing the idea that viewers were listening to the "orchestration of a parallel universe" in the miniseries and season one, the series expanded its unique 'soundscape' in season two by continuing to blend different musical styles and instruments from our world to create a familiar yet completely unworldly score.

"Season two has allowed the show to continue to push the musical boundaries and add new elements to the orchestration," says Bear McCreary, who writes and produces *Battlestar Galactica*'s unique score. "The score to season two included the first season's arsenal of ethnic percussion, Middle Eastern and Asian woodwinds, solo vocalists, ambient synthetic timbres and electric violin, while the Moroccan-inspired acoustic guitars which first appeared in 'Kobol's Last Gleaming' at the end of season one became a much more present sound throughout season two. There were opportunities to introduce electric guitars too, though in a very ambient and ethereal style.

Below: Bear McCreary.

"'Kobol's Last Gleaming' also allowed us to introduce a string orchestra to the *Battlestar Galactica* musical palette," he reveals. "Interestingly, this is the 'color' which has grown the most throughout season two. The challenge for me has been to keep the orchestra interesting and dynamic, and to avoid falling into the trap of traditional science fiction scoring which the producers worked hard to avoid from the beginning. Fortunately, by using delicate orchestration and subtle thematic development, the strings do not distract from the ethnic instrumentation and drums.

"Another thing we did on season two was continue to develop the Celtic instruments of 'The Hand of God'," he adds. "We used a bagpipe and penny whistle combination for the Adama family theme and introduced a solo acoustic violin for Adama and Roslin's theme."

Season two delivered many of *Battlestar Galactica*'s most memorable musical moments and was never short of variety, either. The season's audio highlights ranged from McCreary's superb compositions for 'Pegasus', 'Home' and 'Lay Down Your Burdens' to his rendition of the Phillip Glass piano piece 'Metamorphosis Five'.

"More than anything else, I enjoy the unpredictability of working on this show," McCreary notes. "Every episode is its own little adventure, with new musical styles and instruments being introduced all the time."

Season two's music was co-produced by recording engineer Steve

Kaplan, while the series' principal musicians included Steve Bartek (on guitars), Chris Bleth (woodwinds), M.B. Gordy (percussion) and Paul Cartwright (violin). "I'm very fortunate to have the best production team in the business," McCreary says. "Steve Kaplan creates mixes that have depth and resonate with listeners, and my music has been brought to life by some amazing musicians, whom I have to credit for their invaluable contributions to the show's unique sound.

"I'm also fortunate to have producers and directors with the vision to experiment boldly with music," he adds. "David Eick, Ron Moore and Michael Rymer's musical ideas and willingness to let me experiment have been integral in bringing this fresh approach to scoring to the small screen."

Ultimately, McCreary feels that season two of *Battlestar Galactica* was extremely successful, for both the series and its music. "The greatest achievement of *Battlestar Galactica's* second season was that it fulfilled the promise of the first," he states. "This goes for every aspect of the production and I certainly feel that it applies to the music as well. I am very eager to see where it goes in season three!" ∎

Above: McCreary's scoring of season two has continued to expand the 'soundscape' of *Battlestar Galactica*.

[INTO SEASON THREE...]

"I can see the show becoming even deeper and more complicated and more challenging in season three..." — Ronald D. Moore

Season two of *Battlestar Galactica* saw the series taking another hugely successful FTL Jump forward, both in creative and commercial terms. *Battlestar Galactica* remained the US Sci Fi Channel's top-rated show during the première of its second season and attracted the episodic series' biggest audience to date with its season première, 'Scattered'. The critical response, meanwhile, was arguably even more impressive, as the series won widespread acclaim and numerous accolades for season two. *Rolling Stone* was just one of the many high-profile, mainstream publications that showered praise on *Battlestar Galactica*, calling it "the smartest and toughest show on TV". *Time* magazine went even further, labeling *Battlestar Galactica* "a ripping sci-fi allegory of the war on terror" and naming it as the best TV show of 2005.

Battlestar Galactica's increased success and popularity was reflected in the release of various pieces of official merchandise and spin-off products. Tor Books launched a series of *Battlestar Galactica* novels in January 2006, which began with Jeffrey A. Carver's novelization of the miniseries and *The Cylons' Secret* by Craig Shaw Gardner. Dynamic Entertainment produced a comic-book series based on the new *Battlestar Galactica*, while Hasbro and Art Asylum unveiled a range of *Battlestar Galactica* models and action figures. The series also inspired further soundtrack albums and trading cards from La La Land Records and Rittenhouse respectively, and became the subject of its own bi-monthly newsstand publication with the release of *Battlestar Galactica: The Official Magazine* from Titan.

The American public's awareness of *Battlestar Galactica* was given yet another boost at the start of 2006, when the sci-fi drama became one of the first television shows to be made available to download via iTunes' online store. In the run-up to the series' online début, *Battlestar Galactica* also broke new ground by unveiling the very first iTunes-exclusive video production, the behind-the-scenes documentary *Sci Fi Inside: Battlestar Galactica*.

"*Battlestar Galactica* really landed on the landscape of television in season two," says Ronald D. Moore. "I think the show has changed how people look at science fiction to a large extent and it's opened the eyes of a lot of people — critics, certainly — about what science fiction on television can be. We've shown that science fiction isn't just pure escapist, popcorn-type fare; we've garnered an audience for serious drama in science fiction and have proved you can take this genre seriously and do something relevant to the world we live in and make political and social comment."

By the time season two had finished its première run on Sci Fi in March 2006, the makers of *Battlestar Galactica* all felt proud of what they had accomplished with the series' sophomore year. "I think the show matured in a lot of ways in season two and

we told some great stories," Moore notes. "We produced a lot of really good episodes in season two. I'd say 'Lay Down Your Burdens', 'Pegasus', 'Resurrection Ship', 'Fragged' and 'Flight of the Phoenix' were the real standouts from the year.

"There were only a few episodes I wasn't happy with," he reveals. "'Black Market' and 'Sacrifice' were the two episodes I, personally, was probably least satisfied with. But that's the difference between doing twenty episodes as opposed to thirteen — you can give thirteen episodes more time and tender loving care than you can give twenty. And I think, overall, we were all pretty happy with season two."

Despite any occasional missteps, *Battlestar Galactica* easily remained the flag-bearer for rich and rewarding small-screen science fiction drama in its second season. The series also always looked destined to return for a third season. The show's future was officially confirmed in November 2005 — some three weeks before shooting on season two had wrapped — when Sci Fi announced plans for a twenty-episode third season.

As work began on season three, *Battlestar Galactica*'s cast and crew were all excited about the creative possibilities presented by events in season two's cliffhanging and year-spanning finale, 'Lay Down Your Burdens, Part II'. "I think the end of season two gave us a great starting point for season three," says Moore. "The cliffhanger

Above: Battlestar Galactica's leading lights, Ronald D. Moore (left) and David Eick (right).

changed the formula of the show and changed our character dynamics and relationships, and that gives us a terrific springboard for season three.

"The season begins with the Cylon occupation of New Caprica and it ain't pretty," he continues. "It's great stuff: there's a lot of screwed-up people and they're in a really charged environment. That's giving us a very interesting opening to the season."

"The opening episodes of the season deal with the occupation, the insurgency and the escape," adds David Eick. "We will then be back in space, with our characters trying to reclaim their old lives and positions. That's going to be a very interesting element of the first half of the season."

Season three's story arc also expands on the Cylons' motivations and activities. "We're going to get much more into the Cylon world in season three," Eick reveals. "We're going to get into where the Cylons' belief system comes from and what — if any — hierarchy exists. The challenge for us in doing that will be exploring metaphysical concepts in a way that also maintains *Battlestar Galactica*'s realism."

When *Battlestar Galactica*'s third season began shooting, one thing was for sure: the show's stellar miniseries and opening two seasons were going to be tough acts to follow. This fact wasn't lost on the show's makers.

"Going into season three I have been thinking, 'Oh man, can we do this?'" Moore admits with a grin. "But I've done that at every point on this show; I did it at the end of the miniseries and I had the same feeling going into season two."

"We really don't want to disappoint people with season three and want to maintain the quality of the show — and that's one tall order," Eick agrees. "It is terrifying! But I have to say I'm even more excited and optimistic about what we have planned for season three than I was about the last season. I think we've really found our footing and know how to make this show."

Shortly after the start of shooting on season three, Sci Fi announced that a pilot episode for a *Battlestar Galactica* prequel series was in development. Entitled *Caprica*, the spin-off series takes place fifty years before events in *Battlestar Galactica* and follows the lives of two families — the Graystones and the Adamas — as the people of the Twelve Colonies of Kobol face the birth of the Cylons. *Caprica*'s initial development was spearheaded by Moore and Eick, who enlisted writer/producer Remi Aubuchon (*24, The Lyon's Den*) to work with them on the pilot.

"I think Ron and I started talking about the spin-off during our dinner at Firefly restaurant, when we started planning season two," Eick recalls. "We had a few ideas, but we were so busy on *Galactica* we couldn't really pursue them. It was Universal who suggested that we got Remi involved, because he's a great writer who had pitched an idea to them about the origin of an artificial intelligence, and they said it sounded like the Cylon back-story. So that was how it all began.

"If it gets made, *Caprica* is going to be very different from *Galactica*," he notes. "It's going to be another big departure for the Sci Fi Channel and the sci-fi genre."

BATTLESTAR
GALACTICA

Regardless of what the future would hold for *Caprica*, one thing was clear at the start of *Battlestar Galactica*'s third season: the makers of the series had succeeded in taking the twenty-eight-year-old franchise to unprecedented creative and commercial heights. This fact really came home to the series' head writer/executive producer at the end of 2005, when *Battlestar Galactica* was selected as one of the top ten TV series of 2005 by the American Film Institute (AFI).

"I was just taken aback that we were honored with an American Film Institute Award," says Moore, "and the presentation blew me away. It was a relatively small gathering at the Four Seasons Hotel in Beverly Hills and it was just for the people who were nominated — there were no press or spouses — so it was just myself, David Eick and a few network executives [representing *Battlestar Galactica*]. We went into this room and looked around and it was filled with high-level people like Steven Spielberg, George Clooney and the people who ran *Lost*, and then the doors were shut and they started reading the citations for shows and films.

"It was incredible to hear *Battlestar Galactica* being named by the American Film Institute as a part of America's cultural legacy," Moore declares with pride. "That was a very humbling moment and it was a definite highlight of my entire time on this show.'" ■

Above: Season three of *Battlestar Galactica* will reveal more than ever before about the Cylons.

OWN THE BREAKAWAY HIT BATTLESTAR GALACTICA 2.5!

AVAILABLE ON DVD SEPTEMBER 19

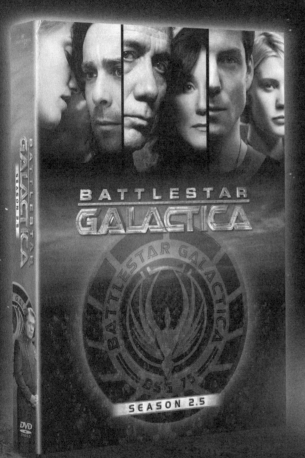

INCLUDES:

- Exclusive Extended Version of The Explosive Midseason Cliffhanger *Pegasus*

- Over **10 HOURS** of Bonus Content

- Presented in Dolby 5.1 Surround Soun

ALSO AVAILABLE

SEASON 1   SEASON 2.0